GOD MOMENTS

GOD MOMENTS

WHY GOD MADE ME PICK UP UNDERWEAR AND OTHER STORIES OF FAITH

ORLANDO U. JAVIEN, JR.

God Moments: Why God Made Me Pick Up Underwear and other Stories of Faith

Interior Book Design by Inspire Books
www.inspire-books.com

Printed in the United States of America

ISBN (paperback): 978-1-950685-18-9
ISBN (e-book): 978-1-950685-19-6

1. Religion / Christian Life / Spiritual Growth
2. Religion / Christian Life / Men's Issues

Contents

Dedication

If I speak with the tongues of men and of angels, but have not love, I am only a resounding gong or a clanging cymbal. If I have the gift of prophecy and can fathom all mysteries and all knowledge, and if I have faith that can move mountains, but have not love, I am nothing. If I give all I possess to the poor and surrender my body to the flames, but have not love, I gain nothing.
1 Corinthians 13:1-3

I dedicate this book to my loving wife, Beth, and my children, Junior and Jennilyn. Without you I would be nothing.

To my parents, I thank you for being great examples of love.

Acknowledgments

The Parable of the Sower

That same day Jesus went out of the house and sat by the lake. Such large crowds gathered around him that he got into a boat and sat in it, while all the people stood on the shore. Then he told them many things in parables, saying: "A farmer went out to sow his seed. As he was scattering the seed, some fell along the path, and the birds came and ate it up. Some fell on rocky places, where it did not have much soil. It sprang up quickly, because the soil was shallow. But when the sun came up, the plants were scorched, and they withered because they had no root. Other seed fell among thorns, which grew up and choked the plants. Still other seed fell on good soil, where it produced a crop—a hundred, sixty or thirty times what was sown. He who has ears, let him hear."

The disciples came to him and asked, "Why do you speak to the people in parables?"

He replied, "The knowledge of the secrets of the kingdom of heaven has been given to you, but not to them. Whoever has will be given more, and he will have an abundance. Whoever does not have, even what he has will be taken from him. This is why I speak to them in parables:

"Though seeing, they do not see; though hearing, they do not hear or understand.

In them is fulfilled the prophecy of Isaiah:

'You will be ever hearing but never understanding; you will be ever seeing but never perceiving. For this people's heart has become calloused; they hardly hear with their ears, and they have closed their eyes. Otherwise they might see with their eyes, hear with their ears, understand with their hearts and turn, and I would heal them.'

But blessed are your eyes because they see, and your ears because they hear. For I tell you the truth, many prophets and righteous men longed to see what you see but did not see it, and to hear what you hear but did not hear it.

Listen then to what the parable of the sower means: When anyone hears the message about the kingdom and does not understand it, the evil one comes and snatches away what was sown in his heart. This is the seed sown along the path. The one who received the seed that fell on rocky places is the man who hears the word and at once receives it with joy. Since he has no root, he lasts only a short time. When trouble or persecution comes because of the world, he quickly falls away. The one who received the seed that fell among the thorns is the man who hears the word, but the worries of this life and the deceitfulness of wealth choke it, making it unfruitful. The one who received the seed that fell on good soil is the man who hears the word and understands it. He produces a crop yielding a hundred, sixty, or thirty times what was sown." Matthew 13:1-23

I would like to thank the supporting cast of this book. First and foremost, I give thanks to the writer and director of this book, my Father, my God, and my Redeemer. I thank you for the mountains and the trees, the sun above my head, and for breath of life. All the glory and praise belong to you.

To my leading lady, my wife, Beth, thank you for sticking by my side and supporting me. You are the inspiration for the chapters on love. To my kids, Junior and Jennilyn, thank you for showing me what childlike faith is. It is such a joy watching you both grow up. "I love you all the time!"

To my mom and dad, the farmers of my life. Thank you for removing the rocks and thorns from my garden and preparing my soil. Mom, thank you for planting so many seeds. Even though the birds came and stole many of them, you continued dropping them along my life's path. Dad, thank you for being the example of servanthood in my life. You have always worked hard to make sure all your kids had a new car and a house to raise their family in, while you drove around in a beat-up car.

To my brothers, sister, and in-laws: Kelvin and Cheryl, Yvonne and Mike, Joseph and Krystal, Johanne, Mackie, and Beth's parents. Thank you for your support and encouragement. Joe, the e-mail that you sent out years ago was the ripple in the water to my journey.

To my nephews and nieces: Alyssa, Justin, Brianna, Kelan, Kyla and Karter. I pray that this book keeps you on the narrow path. "Enter through the narrow gate. For wide is the gate and broad is the road that leads to destruction, and many enter through it. But small is the gate and narrow the road that leads to life, and only a few find it" (Matthew 7:13-14).

To my wrestling coach, Jose Campo, thank you for guidance and instilling in me godly principles.

To all my friends and family that have supported me and forwarded me inspiring e-mails, thank you for thinking of me.

Dr. Matthew Hubbard, the way you run your business and live your life is a true example of living like Christ. Thank you for opening up your home every week for us to worship our Father.

Thank you to the Tuesday morning prayer group, St. Michael's men's group, family Bible study, Cursillo of San Diego, Benedictus of San Diego and Knights of Columbus. I could always count on you to have my back. "As iron sharpens iron, so one man sharpens another" (Proverbs 27:17).

Ryan Tate, thank you for telling me everyone has a story. That comment stuck with me for years, and now here it is.

And finally, I would like to thank Pastor Jurgen Matthesius, Christian City Church San Diego, for convicting my heart with your powerful messages and for baptizing me. Your messages continue to strengthen my faith and bring me closer to the Lord.

Foreword

A life changed, a destiny altered, a vision interrupted, and a soul transformed! This book is the wonderful true story of a human being whose life has the fingerprints of God all over him. In the age we live in today, this post-modern, post-Christian world, where God and belief in God is constantly coming under attack, Orlando Javien Jr. counters with the greatest argument that there is—the testimony of a life transformed by the love and power of Jesus Christ!

There still is only one hope for the world, Jesus Christ! The truth is there is only one way to live, but there are two ways to find out! Living life without God in it leaves one empty and in a constant pursuit of the next thing in an insatiable quest to try to satisfy a longing in the human soul that cannot be satisfied by "stuff" or "things." You cannot fill an eternal longing with a temporal fix, be it a soul mate or financial success or some other noble quest. The Scriptures are true; we were made by God for God, and He truly has "set eternity in their hearts."

May you find the God of peace, love, and life and enjoy these three commodities that only come from him, which the world around us is sadly lacking.

God bless you as you read,
Jurgen Matthesius
Pastor Christian City Church, San Diego

Introduction

There once was a man of many hats. He was a son, husband, father, friend, and employee. On the surface this man seemed pretty normal. He enjoyed watching football games, chugging a few cold ones, and browsing girly magazines. He was a man's man.

Underneath the façade lurked demons hidden to most—demons of selfishness, binge drinking, and an addiction to pornography. That man was me, Orlando U. Javien Jr.

On August 14, 2007, I experienced my "Aha moment!" It was an awakening that would lead to my transformation from a man's man to God's man.

In this book I will share stories of how I found my faith and how I've grown in the past two years. I will share with you my struggles along with my victories in hopes that it will encourage you.

This book is meant for those who have made the confession of faith and need a map to continue their journey with Christ. This book is also meant for the Christian that is struggling with their faith (one foot in the world and the other foot with Jesus). Most of all, this book is meant for the Christian that wants to take their walk to the next level, beyond the ordinary.

I pray that you receive this book for what it is, my testimony of faith.

It Began with an Exorcism

It was on August 14, 2007, that my life changed forever. On that Tuesday morning I mustered enough energy to make it to a 5:00 a.m. prayer group. I was invited weeks earlier, but this was the first one I actually planned to attend. I was expecting to see a few guys reading the Bible and then praying. What I saw instead was profound.

I arrived at Dr. Matt's house just in time for him to inform me that one of their Christian brothers was in trouble and we needed to go to his house. Being my first time, I thought, *Okay, I'm up for it.* We all hopped into Matt's limousine and drove off. I was in the back of the limo wondering what was going on. What really was on my mind was, *I think I'm paying my chiropractor too much money. Who drives around in a limo?*

When we arrived, I met all the other guys in the group and waited to be briefed on the situation. We all gathered in the living room, and John Mower informed us that his house was demon possessed.

All of a sudden it dawned on me that we were there for an exorcism! I was taken aback and thought to myself, *I did not sign up for this!* I couldn't just leave because I rode with Matt.

You may be wondering: *Did John see heads spinning like the movie* The Exorcist? No, but his dogs were barking uncontrollably; he and his wife smelled sulfur around the house; and his wife experienced a being pushing down on her body when she lay in bed.

I didn't need any more explanation than that.

The men in the group took turns praying for the house. We went into each room casting out demon spirits in the name of Jesus. The men in the group were speaking in tongues that I had never heard before. I was in awe with the power and authority they demonstrated.

After it was all over, we went to the limo to leave. I pulled John Moon aside and asked him what had just occurred. He filled me in on the details about speaking in tongues.

On the day of Pentecost all the believers were meeting together in one place. Suddenly, there was a sound from heaven like the roaring of mighty windstorm, and it filled the house where they were sitting. Then, what looked like flames or tongues of fire appeared and settled on each of them. And everyone present was filled with the Holy Spirit and began speaking in other languages, as the Holy Spirit gave them the ability (Acts 2:1-4, NLT)

Then I asked him if I could have the same power that they demonstrated. He got all excited and said, "Yes, all you have to do is except Jesus Christ as your personal Lord and Savior and receive the Holy Spirit."

I thought, *Hey, I've done that before numerous times at church, but I didn't receive any power.* But maybe this time would be different.

John excitedly called all the guys into the limo to pray for me. They all began to pray, and after a few minutes they told me, "You got it; now start speaking." But I couldn't. They kept on insisting I had it but to no avail; I couldn't do it. I realize now it was because I was thinking too hard (head knowledge prevented me from receiving the gift of tongues). However, I did receive the Holy Spirit, and he began a work in me that day. That day a desire was born.

An Awakening

Although the exorcism was the catalyst for me accepting the Holy Spirit, I know it wasn't the only thing. I look back at my journey and see many stepping stones that led me to my current path with the Lord. I believe now that He was always there, only this time I'm actually allowing Him to lead. I may have heard counsel from the Holy Spirit before; I just always chose my own way.

The exorcism was the spark to my faith walk, but the fuel for the inferno to follow was prepared years earlier. It's only through the guidance of the Holy Spirit that I am able to piece all the events together.

Before finding my way to my first prayer group, a series of events occurred. It all started with my son's third birthday party. I was running around and tossing my son up in the air. At one point I bent over to pick him up and tweaked my back. I fell to the floor and felt somewhat paralyzed. I wasn't sure what happened; I just knew it wasn't good.

I lay there for a few minutes until I was able to get up on my own. I felt like an old man (I was only thirty-one at the time). From that day on I was determined to get back in shape. Actually, I was in shape. I was just in the shape of a circle. I'm exaggerating a little bit, but we can be our own worst critics. I just wasn't in my prime.

So in the weeks following, I signed myself up to see a personal trainer. His name was Carlos. He was able to whip me in shape to a certain point. The lower back pain was still hindering me from giving my all to the workouts. Carlos had just started using a new chiropractor, Dr. Matt, and spoke very highly of him. Longing for the freedom from lower back pain, I sought him out.

One morning, Carlos was a little late for our 6:00 a.m. session. He apologized and told me it was because he was at a prayer group with Dr. Matt. I looked at him with amazement and said, "You and a bunch of guys pray at five in the morning? You're kidding me, right?" He wasn't. I left it at that, but I know that statement of faith was a seed planted in me.

So the pieces of the puzzle go like this: First, I hurt my back. Next, Carlos becomes my personal trainer and plants the seed of faith in me that men my age actually take the time to pray. Then Carlos introduces me to my future mentor, Matt.

I had been receiving care from Dr. Matt for approximately six months before asking him about the prayer group he led. I inquired about it because I had accomplished most of the goals I had set out for 2007, except for increasing my faith in God.

Prior to the exorcism I would have classified myself as a churchgoer but not a churchdoer. I was raised in the Catholic church, baptized as a child, and attended church with my family. I really didn't enjoy church growing up except for the fact that I could see my friends and afterwards we went shopping. My dislike came from my lack of knowledge of what was going on and what the messages meant. My mom would always ask me what mass was about so she could find out if I was listening or not. Even when I attempted to listen, I couldn't really remember. Once the message was delivered, I forgot it. I did have the timing of the church down to a science (thirty-five to forty-five minutes into the service we hold hands, shake our neighbor's hands, take the bread, and straight out the door to beat traffic).

After high school I began attending a nondenominational Christian church and seemed to like it better. I was able to understand the messages, and I liked the alter calls. I found peace knowing that if I went up to the altar and confessed my sins then I would be saved from eternal hell. The only problem was after I got home the warm and fuzzy feeling would be gone. I quickly returned to my sinful ways.

My prayers were as pitiful as my church participation. I had a simple prayer that I would recite. I learned it as a child, and it followed me to adulthood. My prayer would go something like this, "Dear God, bless my mom, dad, brothers, sister, aunts, uncles, grandmas, grandpas, cousins, and friends. Forgive me of my sins and those who've sinned against me. And lead me not into temptation but deliver me from the evil one. Amen."

I knew for a fact my knowledge of God was lacking and deserved improvement. I saw that I had been blessed with a beautiful wife, two wonderful kids, a nice home, a loving family, and good job. Now was the time for me to recognize Him.

As I was recognizing the need to know the God that blessed me, I also began enduring a challenging phase in my life.

My wife and I were blessed to be very successful in our careers. At the time my wife was a pediatric nurse and real estate agent, and I was a jack of all trades, master of none. I was a bookkeeper, executive assistant, manager, appraiser, loan officer, and studying to be a real estate agent too. We were juggling all these jobs while raising two kids, one four and the other two. We definitely had a nice house already; however, we both have always dreamed of bigger and better things.

My wife just got her real estate license so she could work on the side, and I was in the process of completing my courses. We were going to team up and make mucho dollars helping people buy and sell homes. At this time, the real estate market was starting to cool off, and our dream home was available at a tremendously lower cost.

So we decided that we would sell our existing house and buy a new one. We had three to four deals in the pipeline and were sure they were all going to close. That would have given us just enough to buy the house and upgrade it with nice wood flooring and custom paint. All we needed to do was sell our house and close all the deals we had on the market.

Talk about stress. We were both spending so much time making more money that we forgot to spend time together. This would lead us to fight constantly because I wasn't giving her the attention she longed for. She would always say to me that I wouldn't communicate or spend time with her. If I did spend time with her, she would tell me that my mind was somewhere else.

I didn't realize that communication was more than just answering her questions. I figured if I answered her questions while watching TV then we were communicating.

My wife also wanted me to spend more time with the kids. She wanted me to play with them and teach them. My idea of playing with them was letting them play around me as I watched TV. I definitely wasn't a candidate for the father of the year award.

My idea of making my wife happy was buying her things that she desired (a house, then an even bigger house). I heard her cry for more attention but always argued back saying I didn't have time to communicate because I was trying to make enough money to buy her the house she wanted or pay off the things we already bought.

I heard her cries for attention but didn't know how to provide it. I read a lot of self-help books, and they did teach me how to love myself more, but when it came down to improving my skills as a husband and father, not so much. My desire to fix my marriage and know the God that blessed me is what ultimately led me to attend the prayer group with my chiropractor.

A week or so after telling Matt I would attend, I saw him at his office and told him, "I'm going to try this week; I just can't wake up that early." He then told me of a man named Craig who traveled from Temecula to his house every week to make the meeting. That is a one-hour drive. That means he would have to wake up at 3:30 a.m. and leave by 4:00 a.m. in order to make it on time. He basically challenged me to come. He hooked me and reeled me in. That week I woke up at 4:00 a.m. to make it. I was actually wide awake and excited to be there.

I arrived at the prayer group a broken and lost soul eager to find answers. I look back and can see that I was at the right place at the right time. The display of power and authority in that exorcism gave birth to a desire in my heart, a desire to know Jesus like those men knew Jesus.

Desire Is Born

You will never make it without desire. The definition of desire is "consuming passion, undying drive, insatiable hunger, unquenchable thirst."
Jentezen Franklin[1]

In my younger days I was on the wrestling team at Mt. Carmel High School in San Diego, California. The adventures I had on the wrestling team are some of my fondest memories that I relive often, especially since my closest friends today were also part of the team.

Although I was on the wrestling team, I wasn't very successful on the mat. Actually, I was pretty bad. My first scrimmage match I won in less than one minute. I took the San Pasqual guy down with a double leg and immediately pinned him with a half nelson. I was victorious that day. I'm sorry to say that was my only victory. My friends always remind me that I spent most of the time counting the lights on the ceiling (that's wrestling jargon meaning I was always pinned).

My lack of success was not due to my lack of skill. Okay, my lack of skill did play a part. However, the main reason for my lack of success was my lack of desire. I wanted to win, I wanted to be a champion, but I didn't have a consuming passion to train like a champion.

While the champions were attending Saturday practices, I chose to go to work. While the champions arrived early to practice, I chose to spend a few extra minutes with my girlfriend. I put money and good times above practice. I can see now why I had no power in wrestling. It was my lack of desire to win.

Desire is the difference between winners and losers. There is no substitute for desire. Jentezen Franklin[2]

On August 14, 2007, a desire to have spiritual power was born. I desired the power that was displayed at the exorcism. I desired it so much that I began downloading messages from the Christian City Church San Diego Web site (www.cccsandiego.com). At home I listened to a message, on my way to work I listened to a message, and during work I listened to a message.

The messages that I heard were nothing like what I had experienced at other churches. The pastor had a cool Aussie accent and intertwined some of my favorite movies into the Gospel. He told stories of how movies like *The Chronicles of Narnia* and *The Matrix* related to Jesus. Because I've always been a movie junkie, I related to what he was talking about. He grabbed my attention with his stories and then motivated me to live a Christ-like life. His messages didn't just leave me with a warm and fuzzy feeling. He convicted my heart and challenged me to make a difference.

Today I've taken it to the next level; I now listen to messages while I sleep. I can't get enough of the Word. Listening to the Word while sleeping is awesome. I go to bed hearing someone say, "God loves me," and I wake up to someone saying, "God loves me."

After the first week of listening to the messages daily from CCC, I wrote this letter:

> August 22, 2007
>
> Dear Friends and Family,
>
> I'm writing this letter today to share a miracle with you. When I first started writing this letter in my head, I contemplated whom I would share this with. At first, I thought to direct it to my family and to those that may be going through the same thing. Then I had a strong desire to share it with as many people as I could.
>
> Throughout adolescence and adulthood, I have heard from my mom, "If you want something, ask God and he will give you the answer." This is what I heard when I asked, "Can I go skiing, can I go play paintball, can I join the wrestling team, and can I go to Vegas or party with my friends?" I always left my mom's side thinking, *How is God going to tell me if I could go or not? Is he going to write a message on my mirror or slip a note in my pocket?* I usually just blew it off by doing whatever I wanted to do.
>
> Over the years I realized that she was right. God does speak to us. Sometimes when I'm in a hurry to start my day at work, I'll find myself forgetting something.

My mind says forget it, I'll get it later, but an inner voice tells me to go back and get it. Usually when I listen to that voice, I'll notice a major accident on the freeway and realize that could have been me.

A long time ago I accepted Jesus Christ as my personal Lord and Savior. I answered the altar call made by the pastor. After receiving salvation, I was ready to share it with everyone. I wanted to go up to my friends and say, "Did you accept Jesus Christ as your personal Lord and Savior? You should, you'll feel great!" Instead, I kept it to myself, afraid that I would be called a Bible thumper. So instead of sharing the Gospel (Good News), I would go back to my sinful ways (lusting, sports betting, and excessive drinking).

Last week I attended a prayer meeting. I again accepted the Holy Spirit into my life. This time I came home and started downloading the sermons from their church. Since that day I've listened to two to three sermons daily, one when I wake up, one when I drive to and from work, and one during work. I've always believed in God, but for the first time I am starting to understand what the Bible is about. I've attempted previously to read the Bible but usually dosed off when Abraham started to begat so and so. So as for those who are familiar with the Bible, I never really got that far. I've always been afraid to give my all to Jesus Christ, but today I'm no longer afraid. The Holy Spirit has entered into my heart and is leading me to share the Gospel of Jesus Christ (the Good News).

Yesterday, God was telling me to get rid of my sinful items (porn). I normally would have a hard time with that, but yesterday I destroyed all of it. At first, I thought why not give it to one of my friends? Then I realized it would be like a drug addict who decided to quit snorting coke and just gave his stash to his buddy. At first, those reading this might say, "God's not talking to you!" However, He proved to me that it was Him talking to me in the messages He sent me that day.

Later in the day, on my way home from work, I turned on one of the sermons that I downloaded. The message was all about ridding yourself of sinful items. At the gym I was on the basketball court and said, "God, if you're really there trying to talk to me, then allow me to make this shot from the three-point line." Sure enough, swish! Now for all those that know about my athletic skills, that's a miracle!

God works in mysterious ways. I used to be shy about sharing my views of God, but what I've learned is, it's not about me. It's all about God and leading people to accept Jesus. I hope you take this letter to heart and help me in my walk with God.

God Bless You All

The letter provoked mixed responses. I got praise from many and jokes poked at me from others. One funny comment I received from my friend Rodney was, "I think somebody hijacked your e-mail!" Overall, I had huge support. Did the letter change anyone? I'm not sure. I look at it as dropping seeds along the path.

A farmer went out to sow his seed. As he was scattering the seed, some fell along the path, and the birds came and ate it up. Some fell on rocky places, where it did not have much soil. It sprang up quickly, because the soil was shallow. But when the sun came up, the plants were scorched, and they withered because they had no root. Other seed fell among thorns, which grew up and choked the plants. Still other seed fell on good soil, where it produced a crop—a hundred, sixty or thirty times what was sown.
Matthew 13:1-8

The following week I wrote and sent out this letter:

> August 27, 2007
>
> Although I'm only thirty-two years old, I've always wondered what the meaning of life was. What is my purpose? In my quest for the meaning of life, I've stumbled across a few good authors, Anthony Robbins and Zig Zigler. For the last five plus years, I've been using their books and tapes to help mold my life.
>
> At the beginning of 2007, I wrote down all my goals that I wanted to accomplish.
>
> - I wanted to improve the relationship with my family
> - Reduce my alcohol consumption
> - Improve my physical fitness
> - Cut back watching TV
> - Receive my real estate brokerage license

- Improve my faith in God

A month ago, when I reviewed my goals, I realized that I had accomplished almost everything on that list.

- Every waking hour I try to spend as much time with my wife and kids
- I've reduced my alcohol consumption
- I've been working out with a personal trainer weekly
- I've reduced my TV time to approximately four to seven hours a week, and they're usually my kids' shows
- I'm two classes and the state exam away from my broker's license

As you can see in my list of accomplishments, it doesn't include improving my faith in God. The point I'm trying to make is that although I've almost completed all my goals, I left out the most important piece (God). With all my accomplishments, I still felt empty inside.

That empty feeling has brought me to where I am today. Wouldn't life be a whole lot simpler if at birth you were given a manual for life? A manual that says this is what you're supposed to do. The funny thing about the question is that there always was a manual (the Bible). I just never bothered to review it. Here are the instructions we were given:

"One day you will stand before God, and he will do an audit of your life, a final exam, before you enter eternity. The Bible says, 'Remember, each of us will stand personally before the judgment seat of God...' Yes, each of us will have to give a personal account to God. Fortunately, God wants us to pass this test, so he has given us the questions in advance. From the Bible we can surmise that God will ask us two crucial questions:

"First, 'What did you do with My Son, Jesus Christ?' God won't ask about your religious background or doctrinal views. The only thing that will matter is, did you accept what Jesus did for you and did you learn to love and trust Him? Jesus said, 'I am the way and the truth and the life. No one comes to the Father except through me.'

"Second, 'What did you do with what I gave you? What did you do with your life—all the gifts, talents, opportunities, energy, relationships, and resources God gave you? Did you spend them on yourself, or did you use them for the purposes God made you for?'

"The first question will determine where you spend eternity. The second question will determine what you do in eternity."[3]

My mom began reaching out to teenagers with this message when I was in high school. I've come to realize that my purpose is to assist her in continuing to spread this message to as many people as possible. Life is still going to have turmoil, sickness, and stress; but these things are a whole lot easier to deal with when you have someone whom you can ask for help, Jesus Christ, our Lord and Savior.

God Bless You All

The past two letters were e-mailed to about 100+ people on my address book. I'm not sure if the letters had any impact other than making the reader feel good for the moment. But as I said earlier, it's just me dropping seeds. I would use the e-mails to start up conversations with family members and friends. The e-mails gave me a way to start the conversation about God. I would say to them, "Hey, did you get my e-mails? What did you think?" If they wanted to know more, then I would engage them in my story. If they didn't, then I left it at that.

You see, as a Christ follower, we are called to spread the Gospel. In Mark 16:15 Jesus says, "Go into all the world and preach the good news to all creation." But not all will listen. Don't be discouraged if they don't. If they will not heed your words, then do as Jesus again commands in Matthew 10:14, "If anyone will not welcome you or listen to your words, shake the dust off your feet when you leave that home or town."

If you desire to share the Gospel to others, then let your story be the witness. Start journalizing how God is working in your life. It's up to you how you will utilize your story. If you desire the courage to step out in faith and be a disciple, then present your desire to the Lord.

I know God will grant your desires because it says so in Psalm 145:19: "He fulfills the desires of those who fear him; he hears their cry and saves them," and in John 15:7, "If you remain in me and my words remain in you, ask whatever you wish, and it will be given you. This is to my Father's glory, that you bear much fruit, showing yourselves to be my disciples."

Passion

Okay, so you've received salvation and made the confession of faith. What's next? How do you keep the fire burning? How do you keep running when you start getting tired? It comes down to one word, *passion*!

Passion is best demonstrated in the intensity of one's training. The great athletes of today, like Lance Armstrong and Tiger Woods, train year round, and it shows in their performances. Lance didn't just get on his bike a few times a week and then win the Tour de France seven times. Tiger didn't just play a few rounds a week and then win fourteen majors. They didn't just try; they prepared to win. They had nutritionists, personal trainers, chiropractors, and massage therapists. They trained their bodies for the trials and tribulations ahead.

Wrestling wasn't the only thing I did half-heartedly. I also tried cross country; I was the slowest on the team. I attempted body-building and took second out of three competitors and later took third out of three competitors. Marathon running would be the next thing I did just to do.

Five years ago, my boss, John, convinced me to run a marathon (26.2 miles). I thought, *I get sleepy driving 26.2 miles.* Not having a hobby at the time, I said why not. So we trained daily after work.

All the magazines I've read on marathons say the body needs to be trained to endure at least twenty miles once or twice before attempting to run 26.2 miles. That's what experts said. Did I listen to the experts? No!

Thirteen miles was the farthest I trained. So when the actual event took place, I died at mile fifteen. My feet were covered with blisters. I was exhausted and now hated running. I was tired of eating gels and drinking Gatorade and just wanted a nice juicy hamburger. I finally finished after walking the last ten plus miles. I was proud of myself for finishing but disappointed that I couldn't run the entire race. My time was five hours and thirty-five minutes.

The second time around, I trained a little harder and ran at least fifteen miles before the race. Conclusion, five hours and thirteen minutes. But I was still disappointed that I couldn't run the whole way. I walked the last six to eight miles.

The third and fourth times actually got worse. I thought experience would produce a better time, but it doesn't matter how much experience you have—without proper training you can't succeed. I was always disappointed because I chose my fate. I had the ability to succeed, but I chose to do things halfway with no passion.

I can honestly say I've lived a very passionless life. I've always done things halfway. But now that I know my goal, I will run my race the way Paul instructed. Paul said in 1 Corinthians 9:24-27:

Do you not know that in a race all the runners run, but only one gets the prize? Run in such a way as to get the prize. Everyone who competes in the games goes into strict training. They do it to get a crown that will not last; but we do it to get a crown that will last forever. Therefore, I do not run like a man running aimlessly; I do not fight like a man beating the air. No, I beat my body and make it my slave so that after I have preached to others, I myself will not be disqualified for the prize.

Forgetting what is behind and straining toward what is ahead, I press on toward the goal to win the prize for which God has called me heavenward in Christ Jesus.
Philippians 3:13-14

Paul is telling us that there is a possibility that we can lose the salvation we received if we don't continue the race. You see, if your purpose is short term, then eventually your training will stop.

When I was preparing for a marathon, I would run at least ten to twenty miles a week in preparation. After the marathon I would take a week to rest. One week would turn into one month, then two and so on. You see, once my purpose was completed, my journey ended.

Many people that seek God usually do so because they have a problem. Maybe it's a marital concern, financial burden, or a health issue. So much effort is put into seeking God in prayer for their problem to be solved. Once the problem is relieved, then their seeking of God stops. If we only seek after God for the blessings, then we will find ourselves quickly departing from Him once we receive it.

So our goal should not be to seek the blessings of God but the God of the blessings. If your purpose is for eternity in the kingdom of heaven, your training will never end.

To remain on fire for God, you must continue to put fuel to the fire (reading the Bible, fellowshipping with other believers, praying, fasting, and giving). I recommend you get an iPod and download messages from dynamic preachers like Jurgen Matthesius; Jentezen Franklin; Nick Vujicic; Matthew Kelly; Father Michael Schmitz; and Father Larry Richards. Listen to them all day and night. In 1 Thessalonians 5:17 it says to pray continually. My way of continuously praying is listening to the Word all day long.

If you want to be a champion for Christ like Tiger is to golf, then you need to train year-round. Praying and reading the Word is like your nutrition. Fellowshipping with other believers is like working out with a personal trainer. Your pastor is like your chiropractor adjusting you and setting you on the right course. And listening to messages on your iPod while sleeping is like a massage—it's relaxing and rejuvenating. All that preparation is for the actual game, the trials and tribulations in life (temptations, personal tragedy, and fear).

So set your purpose on eternity in the kingdom of heaven so that your training will never end.

The passion you need to be victorious in Christ can be seen in the poem below.

The Fellowship of the Unashamed

I am a part of the fellowship of the unashamed. The die has been cast. The decision has been made. I have stepped over the line. I won't look back, let up, slow down, or back away.

My past is redeemed, my present makes sense, and my future is secure. I'm finished and done with low living, sight walking, small planning, smooth knees, colorless dreams, tamed visions, mundane talking, cheap giving, and dwarfed goals.

I no longer need preeminence, prosperity, position, promotions, plaudits, or popularity. I don't have to be right, first, tops, recognized, praised, regarded, or rewarded. I now live by faith, lean on His presence, walk with patience, live by prayer, and labor with power.

My face is set, my gait is fast, my goal is Heaven, my road is narrow, my way is rough, my companions are few, my guide reliable, my mission is clear. I cannot be bought, compromised, detoured, lured away, turned back, deluded, or delayed. I will not flinch in the face of sacrifice, hesitate in the presence of the adversary, negotiate at the table of the enemy, ponder at the pool of popularity, or meander in the maze of mediocrity. I won't give up, shut up, let up, until I have stayed up, stored up, prayed up, paid up, spoken up for the cause of Christ.

I am a disciple of Jesus Christ. I must go till he comes, give till I drop, preach till all know, and work till He stops me. And when

He comes for His own, He will have no problem recognizing me. My banner is clear: I am a part of the fellowship of the unashamed.

—Unknown Author

It's a Guy Thing

One of my biggest struggles in my faith walk was my bondage to pornography and self-gratification. Up until I received salvation, I believed it was normal; I believed it was a guy thing.

At a young age I believed I had a gift of finding the adult magazines in the magazine rack. I don't mean the one on the top shelf. I'm talking about the one that was flipped backwards or stuffed between other magazines. As I grew older, my desires for pornography would escalate from magazines to movies then to adult bookstores and then to strip clubs. The internet revolution would eventually add to the fire. I would scour Web sites for hours looking for the perfect image or perfect scene to watch. I once had hundreds of movies downloaded on my computer. I wouldn't even watch all of them. I just did it in search of the scene that would take me over the edge.

The day I received salvation I wondered why I didn't receive the gift of tongues. Was it because I still had my large collection of pornography? I contemplated whether I was truly saved. Desiring true salvation and spiritual gifts, I deleted all my movies and threw away my collection of video tapes, DVDs, and magazines. Later that day I got confirmation that I did the right thing. The sermon I listened to was all about getting rid of that which caused us to sin.

I felt powerful. I was proud that I had the strength to rid myself of a habit that I had since I was eight. I was set free, but for how long?

After a few months of freedom, I was blindsided. While rearranging a few files on my computer, I came across a video that I had hidden. I prayed for strength to fight the temptation but was too weak. I had already been trapped in the devil's web. I gave in that day. I was satisfied for the moment, but it wasn't long before I felt miserable. I fell to my knees and wept for forgiveness and strength to overcome.

I deleted that video and started all over. That's when I knew I needed help. I asked God for help, and He led me to the book *Every Man's Battle* by Steven Arterburn and Fred Stoeker.

In this book I learned that I was a sex addict. I realized as a sex addict the first step for freedom was admitting I had a problem. I admitted it to my wife and asked her to monitor my internet usage. She was quite disturbed to hear that I had such a problem but was willing to help.

The next step I learned was how to bounce my eyes. You see, I had a staring problem. If I saw a beautiful woman walk by, my mind would go crazy with sexual images. I learned that it is okay to admire the beauty of a woman, but you have to stop there. In 2 Corinthians 10:5 it says that we should take every thought captive and make it obedient to Christ.

Now when my mind starts racing, I immediately say, "Get away from me, Satan!" I make the statement to myself that the girl I'm looking at is my Father's daughter and I will not disrespect Him.

The book also taught me to guard myself. Cable, the Internet, magazines, and adult establishments were my kryptonite. So I cut my cable channels, trashed my collection of movies and magazines, had my wife monitor my internet usage, and avoided adult stores. Also, when the Victoria's Secret catalogue came in, I immediately dropped it into the trash can.

Again, I was victorious, but for how long? This next recovery period was longer than the first but would eventually end. I felt stronger than ever before. The devil was defeated, and I could move on. So I thought. I let my guard down and began opening up the Victoria's Secret magazine before I threw it away. I wanted to test if I was strong enough. The first time I was strong. I looked at it and said, "You have no power over me," and tossed it. The second time I looked at it a little longer than the first. Then in weakness I got on the computer and started searching for some of the movies I viewed in the past. Again, I fell. And again, I was broken and wept for forgiveness.

Now I started wondering how often God would forgive me. Would I run out of chances to repent? That week I went to my prayer group and admitted my sins to my brothers and asked for prayer. I was met with a lot of support because many in the group had similar issues. They all prayed for me that the bondage would be broken off and that I would be set free. After the meeting a new member that came in related to my issue and referred to me a Web site called Setting Captives Free (www.settingcaptivesfree.

com). It is a sixty-day biblical approach to breaking the chains of addiction.

I know that guy was there for a reason. I also realized that I wouldn't have gotten the referral if I didn't lay down my pride and admit my weaknesses. If you desire freedom, then lay down your pride and seek help. The only way to have strength to lay down your pride is through Christ.

I began the Setting Captives Freedom course and was on my way to true freedom. The course taught me that the motivation I have for freedom needs to be for the glory of God. You see, my motivation previously was all about me. I wanted freedom so I could be strong willed. I wanted freedom so I could be saved from eternal hell. I wanted freedom so I could have spiritual gifts. It was all about me. When my motivation is all about me, then I make myself to be an idol. It is a form of self-worship.

If it is all about me, then I am going against God's will. God's will is that whatever I do, I do all to the glory of God (1 Corinthians 10:31).

The course taught me to change the water I was drinking. Previously I was drinking from a well that didn't satisfy. The well that doesn't satisfy was that of pornography. As I said earlier, my desire for pornography grew from magazines to movies and then strip clubs. It continued to escalate. It left me thirsty, wanting more. But the water that quenches my thirst is the living water, which is the Word of God. The Bible is the source that quenches my thirst. It takes more than just reading and listening to the Bible. You must embrace the teachings. By embracing the teachings, you will recognize the lie in the temptation and run away as to not take part in it.

To the Jews who believed him, Jesus said, "If you hold to my teaching, you are really my disciples. Then you will know the truth, and the truth will set you free." They answered him, "We are Abraham's descendants and have never been slaves of anyone. How can you say that we shall be set free?" Jesus replied, "I tell you the truth, everyone who sins is a slave to sin. Now a slave has no permanent place in the family, but a son belongs to it forever. So if the Son sets you free, you will be free indeed."
John 8:31-36

Once I chose the living water, I then had to bring my sin into the light. I was ashamed to tell my wife that I fell again, but the course taught me that by bringing the sin to the light it dies. You see, sin can't live in the light because God is light, and where there is light, there is no darkness (sin).

The next few steps are vital to continuing freedom. First, seek out an accountability partner that will monitor your progress. I asked my wife because I knew she wouldn't go easy on me. Secondly, cut off all sources to that which causes you to sin (the course calls it radical amputation). The first time I just asked my wife to monitor my internet usage. I saw that wasn't good enough and installed a Web filter (www.covenanteyes.com) that blocks inappropriate sites and e-mails my wife what sites I viewed. This is a double wammy because first I will be dinged because the site is blocked then I will get dinged for trying to look at it. It sounds pretty drastic, but it's worth it. Now that I spend less time watching TV and Web surfing, I have more time to spend drinking of God's living water and fostering relationships with my wife and kids.

If you desire freedom from the chains of sin, then seek after God's forgiveness and strength to lay down your pride. Bring your sin to the light and start the course. Be prepared; it won't be easy. The last bit of advice I'd like to impart is don't test yourself. You will lose every time. Maybe not at first, but eventually you will.

Distractions

Enter through the narrow gate. For wide is the gate and broad is the road that leads to destruction, and many enter through it. But small is the gate and narrow the road that leads to life, and only a few find it.
Matthew 7:13-14

The passage above came to me while playing a game called "Brick Breaker." The game is like tennis. You have a paddle that goes from left to right, and you bounce a ball toward bricks. When you hit a brick, it disappears. After you hit all the bricks in the stage, you go to the next level. Every once in a while, hitting a brick will release a bonus (extra life, laser, or multiple balls). The funny thing I noticed was that every time I would chase after the bonuses, I would die soon after.

When I was just concentrating on one ball, I would be fine. When the bonuses would pop up, I would get excited because an opportunity to get ahead presented itself. I would have to time it correctly, hit the ball, chase the bonus, and make it back in time to hit the ball again. When I got distracted, I died.

At first, I was just moving left to right trying to hit one ball. Now I'm trying to hit one ball, catch the bonus, go after the original ball, and press a button to shoot the weapon. A simple game just got complicated.

It's just like life. Most of our original dreams are to get a good job, find a mate, buy a house, have some kids, and live happily ever after. The focus of most Americans today is buying a bigger house, nice cars, and college for their kids. In the chase for the bonuses in life, we neglect our spouses and children. We spend extra hours at the office to pay for the things we bought and for the things that we desire. We try so hard to keep up with the Joneses, not realizing they're buried in debt.

We work forty-to sixty-hour weeks in order to retire sooner. We waste our good years in hopes of having fun when we're older. Now instead of enjoying life, people are miserable, and you can see it in their expressions. That's why many people can't wait for Friday so they can get drunk and forget about their problems. There are many who travel this road because the way is broad and the gate is wide.

I once traveled that same road myself. I worked the long hours trying to get ahead of the game. I would work an eight-hour shift then work another four hours at home. I would only take a break to have dinner with my wife and kids, then back to work. I would dread vacations because I knew when I returned my desk would be full of things to do. In my attempt to lighten the load, I would bring work with me and do it when everyone was sleeping. I also left my phone on just in case someone at the office needed me.

In my attempts to give my wife everything I thought she wanted, I robbed her of her joy. I couldn't give my wife the attention she desired because I thought it was stuff she wanted.

It wasn't until I found the truth in God's Word that I realized I was riding the highway to hell. My hell was drinking half a bottle of scotch every time I fought with my wife, which was quite frequently. I actually counted the days we didn't fight because it was easier.

Why did we fight? The main reason was because we didn't understand each other. My wife wanted more of me while I thought she wanted more stuff. It seems easy enough, but the world's view on how life is supposed to be blinds us.

We communicated less because we knew everything about each other. We didn't have anything else to talk about. The only thing we had in common was our kids. We spent many dinners just staring at each other.

The truth I learned and the changes I made can be seen in my stories on love.

Love Challenges

In my faith walk I've faced a few challenges that I didn't expect. I expected being called a Bible thumper or Jesus freak or falling short of what a true Christian should be. What I didn't expect was opposition from my wife. My wife was receptive to some, but not all, of the changes that I was making.

My wife liked that I watched less TV, consumed less alcohol, led the family in prayer, spent more time with the kids, and eliminated pornography. What she disliked was that I wanted to uproot our family from our current church, and she didn't appreciate all of the extra time I was spending at the men's ministry. She saw the men's ministry as another obstacle to us spending time together.

At first, I couldn't understand why. I mean, most of the changes I was making were to her benefit. This roadblock in my journey troubled me a lot. How was I to continue growing with Jesus if my wife wasn't by my side?

I counseled with a few people, both male and female, and asked them, "Am I doing something wrong?" All the answers I received were, "No, you're doing it right." This troubled me even more. How was I to make my marriage work if I couldn't do anything else to change? My marriage was too important to be right. I needed to find someone to tell me I was wrong.

Sure enough, God led me to *Every Man's Marriage* by Steven Arterburn and Fred Stoeker. I picked up this book, and within the first few chapters I found out that I was wrong. Wow! I've never been so glad to be wrong.

All the changes I was making were good; however, I was still treating my wife the same. I'd become more spiritual, but I was still the same husband that disregarded my wife's feelings. This book opened my eyes to my shortcomings.

Communication was one of my biggest hurdles. It seems I didn't know how. She would always tell me that when I was with her it was like I wasn't there. I couldn't understand it. I was physically there. Wasn't that enough?

Through my readings I learned that communication involves actively listening and actively talking. You need to bounce off ideas back and forth. It's not "just ask a question and answer it." There needs to be substance.

We had grown apart over the years, so I really didn't have a lot to say. I told her all my stories, and she told me all of hers. After we went over our daily work and kids, there wasn't anything else to talk about. We didn't really have any substance to share.

Where do you find this thing called substance? You must seek after it. You see, previously all I did on my free time was watch football, gamble on the internet, and watch pornography. Then when it came time for us to communicate, all I had in my mind was football, gambling, and pornography. As you can tell, there wasn't much detail I wanted to reveal to my wife. So when she would ask, "What did you do all day?" I would reply, "Nothing much."

In order to engage my wife in interesting conversations, I would need to acquire interesting material. I found by reading more and watching TV less I acquired more thought-provoking questions that I could ask her. By reading the Bible I was able to teach her what I had learned. By witnessing to my friends and family, I created stories that I could share. If you want to improve conversations with your spouse, then change what goes in your mind. Remember, garbage in, garbage out.

Along with learning that I had poor communication skills, I also realized that I treated my kids better than I did my wife. If the kids were sick, I would baby them. If they did something wrong, I would forgive them right away. To my wife I would just give her some medicine and tell her to get some rest. If she did something wrong, I would just ignore her. Because she was an adult, I expected her to take care of herself.

The book reminded me that my wife is a treasure given to me by God and I needed to treat her like one. So I began to make her lunch for work, I would call her out of the blue, and I would give her a massage without her asking for it. When I began to treat her like a treasure, she responded by treating me like one also. She would make me a cup of coffee, she would cook my favorite dish, and she would compliment me on my work around the house.

Remember, you wooed your wife to marry you. You should woo your wife to keep her. One of my favorite quotes is "Happy wife, happy life."

Laying down my pride was to be the next step to improving my relationship with my wife. My wife grew up in the Catholic church like I did. When we got married, I led her to Maranatha Chapel, a nondenominational church. I had uprooted her from what she knew, and being a loving wife, she followed. Now that I wanted to move her again to Christian City Church, she wasn't buying it. If we were going to move churches, then it would be to return to the Catholic church.

I had a problem with returning to the Catholic church because I didn't learn anything when I attended one. I didn't realize that my wife actually did. I was being selfish. I was only concerned with what I wanted. To satisfy my wife, we attended a couple of Catholic masses, and I came to the realization that I could learn from the church as long as I listened. We made a compromise and now attend Maranatha Chapel one week and St. Michael's the other week. In this way we both get fed in the manner that we feel comfortable.

Compromise is important in marriage. Remember, it's not all about me; it's all about we.

We are a lot closer now that I've become aware of my shortcomings and have made changes.

I've realized that I was taking my wife for granted. My wife's resistance to my life changes was her way of telling me so. I thank God for my wife's courage to let me see the errors in my way, and

I thank God for leading me to the book *Every Man's Marriage*. If you want a great marriage, get this book, read it with your spouse, and keep pressing forward!

Update: This book was originally published in 2009. In 2010, my wife and I stopped splitting churches and planted ourselves in the Catholic Church.

Desiring to lead my family in the right path I constantly prayed that God would open my wife's eyes to the errors of the Catholic Church. What God did instead was open my eyes to what was right in the Catholic Church.

It was my fervent prayer that God would light a fire upon my wife's heart. What God did was tell me to stop blowing out her flames.

It was my passionate desire to be used in the building of God's Kingdom. What God told me was that it would be done if I allowed it to be done in the Catholic Church.

Perplexed with that call upon my life I took it to prayer and gained the wisdom to accept the call and was confirmed on April 23, 2011.

Going through this experience has allowed me share what I've learned and bridge the gap between my Protestant and Catholic brothers.

Marriage Is Like Golf

With a title like that, I think I grabbed a larger audience of men out there. I sure hope so. Marriage, like golf, is very humbling. I don't play golf all that often, but when I do, it's always the same. At some point in the round, I hit that ball so well it makes me say "Wow! I did that?" Then I do it again and start thinking, *PGA, here comes Orlando Woods.*

Once God hears me thinking that I can do it on my own, he brings me back to reality. The next shot I top the ball, then I totally miss the ball, and to make things worse, I then lose the ball. "PGA, I think not!"

Marriage is the same way. I read a few books (*The Five Love Languages, Every Man's Marriage*, and the instruction book of marriage: Ephesians 5:21) and started to see my marriage improving. Then complacency set in. I stopped showering my wife with love; I thought all the things I did yesterday or last week would carry over to today. Then I was reminded that it doesn't.

I don't get it! What do I need to do to love my wife? I prayed and asked God, "Lord, please show me how to love my wife." Sure enough, he answered quickly. I was led to the book *Fireproof:*

Never Leave Your Partner Behind. I read the book and found the answer I was looking for.

The story was about a firefighter that was so engrossed saving lives that he neglected his marriage. Caught up with an addiction to pornography and only living for himself he forgot about the special gift that he had in a wife. The book taught me that whatever you put the time, energy, and money into will become more important to you.

I'm not good at golf because I don't practice. If I don't continuously practice loving my wife, I won't be good at loving her either. So practice loving your wife. Get books on how to better love them and don't get complacent. Remember, you wooed her to get her; you better woo her to keep her.

Faith—God Made Me Pick Up Underwear

Jesus told them, "I tell you the truth, if you had faith as small as a mustard seed, you could say to this mountain, 'Move from here to there,' and it would move. Nothing will be impossible for you."
Matthew 17:20 (NLT)

The mustard seed in the Bible represents faith. I believe faith is compared to a seed because, like a seed, faith needs to grow. A seed doesn't just become a tree, just like I didn't all of a sudden become a bold Christian. Both take time to develop. As the seed grows into a tree, so your faith grows to allow you to fully surrender your life to Christ.

After I received salvation, I began to actively seek the voice of God. I would ask God to speak to me and give me some direction. I kept on expecting to hear an audible voice, but instead I heard an inner voice guiding me. The first thing I noticed God telling me was to pick up the trash on the ground. I thought, *Huh, is that you, God?* Whether it was Him or not, I figured that's not that hard to do, and if it is Him, then I guess I'm being obedient.

Next, God led me to put away shopping carts, not just mine but the stray ones that were blocking parking spaces. It was actually starting to bug me. I couldn't go anywhere without picking up trash or putting away shopping carts. But I realized, I had prayed for God to speak to me, and He was. He was just testing me in the small things before He could trust me in the bigger things.

Consider it pure joy, my brothers, whenever you face trials of many kinds, because you know that the testing of your faith develops perseverance. Perseverance must finish its work so that you may be mature and complete, not lacking anything.
James 1:2-4

Sure enough, God saw my faith in the small things, so He started to trust me with the bigger things. That's when he asked me to pick up underwear!

I just got out of the gym one morning. I parked to the right, but for some reason I walked to the left. There it was, underwear. I looked up to God and said, "No, that's different; that's underwear!" I started to walk away, until I became so convicted that I said, "Okay, I'll do it!"

When you ask God to speak to you, be ready to listen and obey; otherwise, He may not be willing to use you. So I went to my car, grabbed a plastic bag, and picked up the underwear. I threw it away and said to myself, "Ha ha, very funny, God. I know you're going to reward me today."

It's important to realize God rewards his obedient children as seen in the passage from the book of Hebrews. "And without faith it is impossible to please God, because anyone who comes to him must believe that he exists and that he rewards those who earnestly seek him" (Hebrews 11:6).

He did reward me that day. The company I worked for received a large check in the mail. The check meant I was able to cash my paycheck. I looked up in the sky and said, "Thank you!"

The little tests of faith began to grow even bigger, as you will see in my next two stories.

The Running Evangelist

One of my favorite things to do is run around Miramar Lake. One Saturday morning was no different; my wife pushed the kids in the stroller while I took off running. I was still trying to get back in shape, so running fast was out of the question. I was winded after only one mile, so I decided to take it easy and enjoy the scenery. I marveled at what God created: the beautiful trees, the majestic mountains, the bright blue sky, and the calming waters. I thanked the Lord for the cool breeze as the sun was beginning to overpower the clouds.

I figured since I wasn't running fast, I would say hi to everyone I encountered. I motivated those who were looking exhausted by cheering them on or telling them they were doing a good job. I put on a big smile hoping it would cause others to smile too. I got some to smile back, and others just passed me by without noticing. No big deal, I was just dropping seeds.

You are the light of the world. A city set on a hill cannot be hidden. Neither do people light a lamp and put it under a bowl. Instead they put it on its stand, and it gives light to everyone in the house. In the same way, let your light shine before men, that they may see your good deeds and praise your Father in heaven. Matthew 5:14-16

That is my desire, to have God's light shine so brightly from me that everyone I encounter will know I was in the presence of the Almighty Father.

Toward the end of the run, I felt strong enough to run faster. I figured since I only had one more mile to go, I might as well just try to kick up the tempo and finish. A quarter of a mile into the faster tempo, I realized that I might pass someone who actually needed encouragement, so I slowed down.

As I was running faster, I remembered passing a family with a disabled girl riding in a stroller. God put it on my heart to go pray for her. I started to doubt God. More likely, I started to doubt myself. I was afraid that they would be offended. I was jogging in place for a few moments and looked up at God and remembered that as a Christ follower, I'm led to pray for the sick.

Jesus said to, "Heal the sick, raise the dead, cleanse those who have leprosy, drive out demons. Freely you have received, freely give." Matthew 10:8

I was convicted at that point. I knew if I disobeyed God, He might lose faith in me to do His will. I also thought again I needed to increase my faith, because at that point I had not yet received the gift of tongues. So I doubled back and approached the mom. She looked at me and asked what I wanted. I told her my name and that God led me to pray for her daughter. She was surprised and then questioned my faith. After I told her I was a Christian, she allowed me to pray for her daughter.

Because I was still young in my faith, I didn't really know what to pray for. I prayed for God to comfort her and her family. Very short, but it was all I knew to pray for. I was just trying to be obedient.

They said, "Thank you," and I was on my way. My reward was warmth in my heart. God showed me that He cares for His children and He sends us to show His love.

Praying for International Subcontractors

I know God will not give me anything I can't handle. I just wish that He didn't trust me so much.
Mother Teresa

Again, I went out on an early morning run. To kill two birds with one stone, I prayed for all the houses I passed. I exercised my heart and my spirit. I was almost home when I passed a group of international subcontractors. After I passed them, God put it on my heart to pray for them. Again, I started to doubt my ability to approach complete strangers. I started jogging in place and remembered my morning prayer to God was to use me. Sure enough, when you desire things of God, He answers pretty quickly. You just have to be willing to listen.

But blessed are your eyes because they see, and your ears because they hear. For I tell you the truth, many prophets and righteous men longed to see what you see but did not see it, and to hear what you hear but did not hear it.
Matthew 13:16-17

When anyone hears the message about the kingdom and does not understand it, the evil one comes and snatches away what was sown in his heart.
Matthew 13:19

I was convicted and ran back to the group of workers. There were about twenty plus people getting ready to start landscaping the park. I approached one guy and asked if I could pray for him and his friends. He told me he didn't understand English and directed me to someone else. The next guy I approached seemed like he was looking for approval of his friends. Determined to pray whether they wanted it or not, I spread out my arms and prayed for them all. I prayed that God would bless their workday and give them shade from the heat. I then directed them to do the same to those who missed the prayer. I wonder if they understood me. I'm not sure how they received the prayer, but I did what I was instructed to do.

The Bible instructs us to pray for others, and if it's not received then go on your way.

If anyone will not welcome you or listen to your words, shake the dust off your feet when you leave that home or town.
Matthew 10:14

After I left, I looked up at God and said, "Thank you for increasing my faith. Thank you for the courage to speak to your children."

Losing My Job

As I wrote this book, I had confronted a new challenge in my life. In a time when thousands of people were losing their jobs, I was informed that I too would be joining the unemployed. I lost a job that I had worked at for almost fourteen years.

After looking at job postings on the internet, I became very discouraged. There I was, a man that never had to fill out a résumé looking for a job, in a time where there were 1,000 people applying for one position. I scrolled through each job post until I found something I liked. I was quickly disappointed to find out all the jobs I qualified for or wanted only paid ten to twelve dollars an hour. Doh!

Then I found other jobs that paid more, but the minimum requirements were frightening. All the abbreviations on the qualification sections were foreign to me. I had no idea what ACT, CSI, SQL, CAT, DOG, or BUG meant.

I talked to my buddy Eric about my frustration. He put it to me like this, "It's like you just broke up with the girl you've dated for fourteen years and all of the sudden you have to start dating again. You're not sure whether you should take her to the movies, buy her flowers, or hold her hand on the first date." It was pretty funny.

The first few days of unemployment were good. I knew that if God closed one door, He would open up a bigger and better door for me. "God will provide," I told myself. But I'm human; doubt and fear popped up in my head. I just couldn't keep from hanging my head down in distress. I said to God, "I know you're there. I'm getting a little scared over here; help me please!"

Within a few minutes I turned on the TV, and before the picture showed up, I heard the word *doubt*! I was taken aback. How did Jesse Duplantis know that I was thinking about doubt? His message was about stopping the devil's words from taking root in our heart. You see, if a thought comes to us, it first enters the mind; then if allowed, it enters and plants itself into the heart.

That's why we must "take captive every thought to make it obedient to Christ" (2 Corinthians 10:5). We need to take the word *doubt* and rebuke it before it can take root into our heart. We need to speak the word of God, saying, "For God has not given us a spirit of fear and timidity, but of power, love, and self-discipline" (2 Timothy 1:7 NLT).

How can you truly know you have faith if you are never tested? A man must be tested in order to get stronger.

So be truly glad. There is a wonderful joy ahead, even though you have to endure many trials for a little while. These trails will show that faith is genuine. It is being tested as fire tests and purifies gold. So when your faith remains strong through many trails, it will bring you much praise and glory and honor on the day when Jesus Christ is revealed to the world.
1 Peter: 1:6-7 (NLT)

When there is a drought, a tree will dig its roots deeper into the ground to find water, which makes its foundation stronger. So I too must dig deeper to strengthen my foundation of faith. If you are facing similar challenges, then welcome them as opportunities to strengthen your faith muscles. Remember, God says in His word that He will never forget you.

"Never will I leave you; never will I forsake you." Hebrews 13:5

Look at it as a stepping stone to God's plan for you.

God Rewards the Obedient

I had a feeling I was going to get laid off. It wasn't an issue of if; it was an issue of when. You see, my job was bookkeeper and financial advisor to the CEO. Months earlier I presented my boss with a forecast of the next few months. The numbers were outright ugly. I put together a report offering cost cutting measures needed to survive. In my analysis, I included a breakdown of my brother's and my salary. I made recommendations where cuts could be made, but I told him the fate of my brother and I would be up to him. Our income was a personal issue, and I couldn't make that decision. I thank God that he decided to keep us both for a few more months.

A week prior to the layoff, I mentioned to my prayer group that my job was in jeopardy. The men prayed that God would open new doors for me. As I was leaving, one of the new members, Greg, approached me. He mentioned that his wife needed some help with her bookkeeping business.

I didn't have to fill out a résumé or have an interview. God just said, "Here you go; your obedience in me has been recognized, and this is your reward." He was preparing to close one door, and He already had another one open.

This layoff is no doubt a blessing from God. Now I get to work from home and be around my family even more. I was once a workaholic. I was captive to my job, but the Lord set me free. Although the income is much lower, the reward is greater. You can't buy back the youth of your kids. It's priceless.

God has already begun to use my job loss for his glory. My wife, who has openly admitted to not knowing a lot of Bible verses, said to me the other day, "God says don't despair for he has great plans for the righteous." She even sent me this e-mail that made me fall in love with her even more. With her permission, here it is:

> My dearest husband,
>
> With the challenges and adversities that we are currently undergoing in this chapter of our life, I'd like to share this with you…
>
> "Life is not about waiting for the storms to pass . . . it's about learning how to dance in the rain!
>
> It's how we react to those challenges and adversities that will determine the joy and happiness in our life. During tough times, do we spend our time feeling sorry for ourselves, or can we, with gratitude, learn how to dance in the rain?
>
> When we focus on being grateful for the abundance that's present and not what's missing from our lives, we experience heaven on earth."[1]
>
> ~it's all about perspective~
>
> Your loving wife,
> Beth

Besides the increased time I now have with my wife and kids, the loss of my job has created some great opportunities. I've been able to finish this book that you are now reading; I now have the opportunity to practice everything I learned from the great sales gurus, Anthony Robbins and Zig Ziglar; and I am also personally ministering to my friends and family more.

At this present time, I am building a bookkeeping and tax practice along with slowly growing my speaking business. In addition to the two businesses that I'm building, I also created the newsletter, "The Javien Chronicles" and am a regular creator on YouTube and Linkedin. My hope is that, through my content, those around me may live purpose-driven lives. If you wish to receive this free newsletter, go to orlandojavien.com and click on the newsletter button.

In addition to personally ministering to my friends and family, my wife and I have begun monthly prayer meetings with our family. My vision for the future is to tour the nation telling my story to thousands of people. In order for me to reach thousands, I must first learn how to reach a few.

You see, if you accept the challenges that come your way as stepping stones to success, then you can find peace in any challenge. God wants to use you if you will be willing to let Him to put you in the refiner's fire.

For he will be like a refiner's fire or a launderer's soap. He will sit as a refiner and purifier of silver; he will purify the Levites and refine them like gold and silver.
Malachi 3:3

You see, a refiner must put silver in the hottest part of the fire to remove all the impurities. He will know that the silver is ready when he can see his own image in it. God refines us like silver. He allows us to enter the hottest fire of life in order to remove the impurities. He keeps us in the fire until He can see His image in us. So don't be afraid if you are in the fire; He is trying to make you in His image.

The Power of the Tongue

Death and life are in the power of the tongue...
Proverbs 18:21 (AMP)

In our culture today we take the words that come out of our mouths so lightly. We could accomplish so much if we would just harness the power that it holds. When God created the earth, all he said was, "'Let there be light,' and there was light" (Genesis 1:3). We too have the power to speak things into existence like death and life.

Why did God say death before life? It's because speaking negatively, or death, is natural, while speaking positively, or life, is unnatural. I have to choose to speak positively. I don't have to teach my kids to say bad things, but I do have to teach them constantly how to be polite and respectful. It's not an easy concept to grasp; that's why many spend millions a year on motivational programs.

That leads me to *Get To* vs. *Have To*. One morning, I watched my wife frantically searching for her eyeglasses and taking her last swig of coffee before she headed off to work. In her haste, she said something like this in a solemn tone, "I have to go to work." I noticed her frustration and wanted her to leave with a smile.

I hugged and told her to instead of saying, "I have to go to work," say, "I get to go to work." I told her to try it out to see if it improved her attitude. She wasn't buying it, so I started kissing her and said, "What sounds better, 'I have to kiss my wife,' or, 'I get to kiss my wife!'; 'I have to love my wife,' or 'I get to love my wife!'" She got the idea, and it put a smile on her face.

I utilize the same concept with my kids when its time to get ready for school. I tell them, "You guys get to go to school today!"

"Have to" is such a disempowering phrase. If you put "have to" in front of any action, it automatically makes it a chore; but if you put "get to" in front of the same action, you automatically make it an activity.

I don't have to preach the Gospel. I get to!

Perspective Is Key

Speaking positively, like I said earlier, isn't easy. It needs to be learned and applied. The most important part of speaking positively is perspective, being able to see a situation through different viewpoints. My wife has always told me, "Look at the situation from my point of view or try walking in my shoes for once." If I choose to only look at a situation through my own eyes, then I won't be able to see the whole picture.

Once you learn the importance of seeing through different eyes, then you need to have the discernment to choose which viewpoint is positive and which is negative. Then choose the positive one.

When I was laid off of work, I could have easily been bitter. I could have said, "Why me?" Instead I chose to say to my boss, "Thank you for giving me the opportunity to serve you all these years. Thank you for teaching me so much about business." I chose to speak life into the situation instead of death.

When I get in an argument with my wife, I need to look at it as another opportunity to make up. When the devil comes to attack me, I say, "My Father God said you were coming; your attack reassures me that God's word is true."

When you can speak life into every situation, you will have peace of mind. That's why we shouldn't be roaming this earth in despair and waiting to find peace in heaven. The Lord's Prayer says, "Our Father in heaven, may your name be kept holy. May your Kingdom come soon. May your will be done on earth, as it is in heaven" (Matthew 6:10 NLT). God tells us that we can have heaven on earth. Why wait until you die to have peace?

Your perspective comes from what you allow to enter your mind and who you associate with. If I were to watch the news every day while unemployed, I would be depressed. Every day they are reporting more job cuts, and thousands of people are applying for one job opening. I heard a story the other day that five hundred plus people were applying for one janitorial job. I only watched for a few minutes and changed the channel. If I exposed myself to that daily, then my perspective would be negative. I'd have the belief that I would never get a job. So instead of watching the news, I would just ask someone in the waiting room or in a line if I missed anything. It is a great way to strike up a conversation.

If you're a single man thinking about marriage, don't hang around a bunch of divorced men. They'll tell you marriage sucks! You'd be grabbing on to the wrong perspective. Seek out married men that know it's hard work but wouldn't trade it for the single life, ever.

"He who walks with the wise grows wise, but a companion of fools suffers harm" (Proverbs 13:20).

If you want the right perspective, then hang around those that have the perspective you want. If you want to be successful, then hang around those that don't see a recession but an opportunity.

If you want to grow spiritually, then hang around prayer warriors that see the devil's attacks as a chance to kick his butt. Remember, you become what you surround yourself with.

The Enemy Comes to Attack

Stay alert! Watch out for your great enemy, the devil. He prowls around like a roaring lion, looking for someone to devour. Stand firm against him and be strong in your faith. 1 Peter 5:8-9 (NLT)

Walking with the Lord is not easy. Living in Christ is the hardest thing to do. When you are living in the world, you can lust over women and say it's a guy thing. You can lie and justify that you didn't hurt anybody. Or you could steal and say it was just a small thing.

When you're of this world, you live according to the world's standards. Standards that say the Ten Commandments are just suggestions. When you live in Christ, the Ten Commandments are magnified. Now that ream of paper you took from the office makes you feel so guilty that you put it back; or when you lust over a girl, you feel ashamed because you committed adultery in your heart; or that little lie stirs something inside you to tell the truth. It's not easy, but the reward is great. The reward is reassurance that you will spend eternity with your Father, your God, and your Redeemer.

When you decide to follow Christ, you become the number one enemy to the devil. The devil doesn't want you to seek and save the lost. The devil wants you to do whatever you want to do. He wants you to do anything that is opposite of God's will for you.

It is very necessary to learn early in the Christian walk that there will be trials and tribulations. It's not just a walk in the park.

"But a time is coming, and has come, when you will be scattered, each to his own home. You will leave me all alone. Yet I am not alone, for my Father is with me.

I have told you these things, so that in me you may have peace. In this world you will have trouble. But take heart! I have overcome the world."
John 16:31-33

We also glory in tribulations, knowing that tribulation produces perseverance…and character.
Romans 5:3 (NKJV)

So be truly glad. There is wonderful joy ahead, even though you have to endure many trials for a little while. These trials will show that faith is genuine. It is being tested as fire tests and purifies gold. So when your faith remains strong through many trials, it will bring you much praise and glory and honor on the day when Jesus Christ is revealed to the whole world.
1 Peter 1:6-7 (NLT)

The day I prayed for the international subcontractors, I got in a big fight with my wife. I was blindsided. I came home and was excited to tell my wife what I did. At first, she was proud and amused by me.

She started to get ready for work. I followed her downstairs and prepared her a cup of coffee. Right before she left, we got in a huge argument. I can't remember why, but it came from nowhere.

I didn't get it; I should have received a reward, not punishment. I fell to my knees to pray and asked God for wisdom and discernment. Then I realized that the devil was trying to stop my progress. He wanted me to believe that my reward for praying for the subcontractors was punishment.

It was only through my understanding of the Word that I knew that the devil attacks those that are doing the will of God. So I immediately texted my brothers in Christ and asked for prayer. This is what I sent them: "The devil prowls around like a roaring lion looking for someone to devour. Brothers put on your whole armor of God and pray with me."

I saw the attack and assembled my soldiers to fight with me. I then texted everyone on my phone, "God Bless You."

The enemy attacked me with one arrow, and I blocked it with the shield of faith and struck back with one hundred plus arrows of love and encouragement to my friends. I then prayed for my son's teacher, Mrs. Maria, who was battling an illness.

That day when I got to work, my coworker Gaby asked me how I knew she needed encouragement. She had just revealed something that she'd been hiding for years to her mom. She told me the text gave her reassurance that she did the right thing. Now the two have a stronger relationship.

Another recipient was my brother-in-law, Mike. He said he received the text right before an exam. He ended up acing the test.

I also received a couple of replies later asking who texted them, "God Bless You!" I guess I had their number, but they didn't have my name saved on their phone. That one text helped me reconnect with some old friends. Now I get to minister to those I lost touch with too. I have even received texts from nonbelievers out of the blue saying, "God Bless You."

The devil tried to attack me, but the Lord was able to use the attack for His glory. We can only defeat our enemies when we realize who they are (the world, the flesh, and the devil).

For we do not wrestle against flesh and blood, but against principalities, against powers, against the rulers of the darkness of this age, against spiritual hosts of wickedness in the heavenly places. Ephesians 6:12 (NKJV)

Now that we know whom we are fighting against (the world, the flesh, and the devil), we need to know how to defeat them.

We must "take up the whole armor of God, that you may be able to withstand in the evil day, and having done all, to stand.

Stand therefore, having girded your waist with truth, having put on the breastplate of righteousness, and having shod your feet with the preparation of the gospel of peace; above all, taking the shield of faith with which you will be able to quench all the fiery

darts of the wicked one. And take the helmet of salvation, and the sword of the Spirit, which is the word of God; praying always with all prayer and supplication in the Spirit, being watchful to this end with all perseverance and supplication for all the saints—and for me, that utterance may be given to me, that I may open my mouth boldly to make known the mystery of the gospel, for which I am an ambassador in chains; that I may speak boldly, as I ought to speak.
Ephesians 6:13-20 (NKJV)

Take Away the Devil's Punch Line

A joke without a punch line stinks! My buddies from high school can sometimes have a sick sense of humor. They relish in making fun of each other's flaws, like loss of hair or double chins. My buddy Eric taught me that the best way to deflect ridicule is to admit your flaw before they have a chance to make fun of it.

For me, I have been known to drop a football a few too many times, and my dancing is pretty bad. So by openly admitting these things before the jokes start, it eliminates their ammunition against me, and they will go after other prey.

The devil is the same way. "He prowls around like a roaring lion, looking for someone to devour" (1 Peter 5:8 NLT). The devil tries to plant in our head that we can't minister to the lost because we are full of sins ourselves. We may have been captive to lust, pornography, or lying. The devil says, "You can't win anyone; who is going to believe a tainted sinner like you?" He wants to plant the seed of doubt in your head. He wants to hinder your progress.

But if we would just lay down our pride and openly admit our transgressions, we could be great witnesses of Jesus Christ. I am a great witness to being set free of pornography and self-gratification.

I am a great witness to how Christ could repair a failing marriage. If I kept those struggles and successes in my life secret, then it only benefits me. But when I share my struggles and successes with others, then to God be the glory. So examine yourself. Try to find the issues that you've faced and conquered through Christ and share them so that you too will attract more to God's kingdom.

He-Man

He-Man was one of my favorite cartoon characters growing up. His heroic character would only come out when he needed to fight. When duty called, Prince Adam would unsheathe his sword, raise it up in the air, and say, "By the power of Grayskull…I have the power!" Then he would become the mighty He-Man and defeat Skeletor and his henchman.

As a warrior in God's army, we are similar to He-Man. When we're not fighting the devil, we are just going on with our daily tasks walking around like normal folks. But just like Prince Adam, when duty calls, we call upon the sword (the Word of God) and defeat the devil and his henchmen.

I've noticed when I fight with the devil, I become very exhausted. It's as if I had a physical fight. I've come to the conclusion that the exhausted feeling comes because not only did I fight but I also spent many hours awaiting the fight.

I've always been in the defensive position trying to prevent the touchdown. The problem is that my defense wasn't getting enough rest. So from now on, instead of waiting for the devil to attack me, I bring the fight to him first. I do this by constantly witnessing to my friends and family. I do this by handing out powerful sermons that I listened to. I just make a few copies and carry them wherever I go. I give them to the bankers I meet, the parents at my kids' school, and my family members. It is a great icebreaker to witnessing to someone.

I just hand them the DVD and say, "I want you to check this out! It's an awesome story!" Don't say anything else. This way you qualify your prospect. Their response will determine if they are open to you sharing the Gospel with them. I think we try so hard to witness that we end up overwhelming them with data. Remember K.I.S.S., Keep It Short and Sweet.

Another way I take the fight to the devil is to listen to the Word of God all day long. You may think it's overboard, but I listen to messages almost ten to twenty hours a day. I listen when I'm working, while I'm driving, and while I'm sleeping. I do it because it's God's instructions. If you have ever put something together, you know what happens when you don't follow the instructions. God gives us instructions because He knows what will be going through. So follow Him.

But his delight is in the law of the Lord, and on his law he meditates day and night. He is like a tree planted by streams of water, which yields its fruit in season and whose leaf does not wither. Psalms 1:2-3

Praying continually keeps the devil on his toes. It doesn't allow him to get his offense ready for the next play. You are basically blitzing him on every play.

The weapons that you receive don't just magically fall into your lap; you receive them by reading and absorbing the Word. Then you utilize them by saying the words with faith, believing that they will come to pass.

When the devil tries to attack you, say to him, “No weapon formed against [me] will prosper!” (Isaiah 57:17 NKJV).

When your finances are attacked, say to the devil, “And my God shall supply all [my] needs according to His riches in glory by Christ Jesus!” (Philippians 4:19 NKJV).

And when fear strikes, say to the evil one, “For God has not given [me] a spirit of fear, but of power and of love and of a sound mind!” (2 Timothy 1:7 NKJV).

It has been said that the person that throws the first punch will win the fight. So I say to you stop waiting for the devil to attack you. Take the fight to the devil.

Authority

"You work for my dad, right? Go get me McDonald's." Those words were said to me by my boss's four-year-old daughter, Courtney. This little girl said it with such authority because she knew who her father was. Her dad was my boss, and when he asked me to get food, I would return with McDonald's.

Courtney understood the authority of her father, and she believed since she was under the authority of her father then she had authority over me. The best demonstration of authority in the Bible is seen by the Roman centurion.

When Jesus had entered Capernaum, a centurion came to him, asking for help. "Lord," he said, "my servant lies at home paralyzed and in terrible suffering." Jesus said to him, "I will go and heal him." The centurion replied, "Lord, I do not deserve to have you come under my roof. But say the word, and my servant will be healed. For I myself am a man under authority, with soldiers under me. I tell this one, 'Go' and he goes; and that one, 'Come,' and he comes. I say to my servant, 'Do this,' and he does it."
Matthew 8:5-9

This centurion understood that he had the power over man because he had the backing of the Roman Empire. He also understood that Jesus was under the authority of His Father, God, and had power over the spiritual realm.

Then Jesus said to the centurion, "Go! It will be done just as you believed it would." And his servant was healed that very hour. Matthew 8:13

The centurion received his reward because he honored Jesus and understood authority. When you fully submit your life to Christ, you too will inherit the authority of Jesus. When you submit your life to Christ, you die to self and Christ lives through you. When the devil comes attacking, all you need to do is stand your ground and in the name of Jesus rebuke him. Speak to the devil as Jesus did, "Get behind me, Satan! You are a stumbling block to me" (Matthew 16:23).

You as man do not have the power to rebuke the devil, but Christ in you does. The devil will depart from you because he too is under the authority of Christ. So I say to you today: die to self and live in Christ. You die to self when you put your worldly desires aside to take on the desires of God. You die to self when you say, "I have been crucified with Christ and I no longer live, but Christ lives in me" (Galatians 2:20). It's no longer about me and now it's all about God.

God Calls Me Daily

My cell phone gets bombarded with solicitation and fake calls almost daily. It can get very aggravating. At one point in time I contemplated changing my cell number. Then I got an idea. The numbers were always the same, so I saved the number to my phone and labeled the phone number "God is Love." Now every day out of the blue, I get a phone call from God. Another number I labeled "U R an Overcomer in CJ (Christ Jesus)." So now instead of getting frustrated from the solicitations or crank calls, I get a call from God daily. "

You may hear people say, "God gave me this sickness so I could find Him." That's not true; sickness is a spirit of the evil one. But God can use that sickness for His glory by helping you find Him in the sickness. God uses what was meant for evil for good.

You intended to harm me, but God intended it for good to accomplish what is now being done, the saving of many lives.
Genesis 50:20

So I turned the unwanted calls that used to irritate me into phone calls that make me smile, phone calls that remind me that God is always with me. That's the key to living in Christ. You turn the irritating into the glorifying.

To Seek and Save the Lost

Most of my life I've been trying to find my purpose. I've actually been contemplating the meaning of life since I was in my early twenties. I started writing a book on the subject at age twenty-one. I didn't really get too far, probably because I hadn't experienced life yet.

Now that I've put on a few years, I have a lot more to say. Up until August 2007, I didn't really have a purpose. I mean, I had a good job; I was married and had two kids. Other than being a husband, dad, and employee, I didn't really have a purpose.

Once I got saved and began reading books on purpose, I realized that the purpose of every Christian is to seek and save the lost. That made things easier. My purpose was handed to me. I didn't have to search anymore.

I didn't want go out on the streets and start evangelizing because I wasn't properly equipped. I hadn't memorized many verses, nor did I know the proper way to witness. So I chose to just tell my story to my friends and family via my website, www.orlandojavien.com. I figured instead of trying to shove religion down people's throat, I would tell people my story in hopes of it stirring the same desire in them.

For the first few months, my Web site received lots of applause but no salvations. I enjoyed the praise, but I wanted to save eternal lives.

As I began to gain more knowledge, I started personally witnessing to individuals that showed an interest in my journey. After sharing my story, I would always ask if they wanted to accept Jesus as their personal Lord and Savior; most of the time they would.

So I would lead them in the salvation prayer and would then instruct the new convert to read their Bible and go to church regularly. After allowing some time to pass, I would follow up to see how they were doing in their journey. I would always be disappointed to see that they didn't have the same desire that I had.

Because of the lack of real salvations, I went searching for answers. Was I doing something wrong? I asked the Lord for answers, and sure enough, because my desires were in line with His, He answered quickly. That's when I was introduced to "Hell's Best Kept Secret" by Ray Comfort. You can listen to the message for free on his Web site, www.wayofthemaster.com.

The message of *Hell's Best Kept Secret* teaches a more effective way to offer salvation to others. Salvation is usually offered as a way to get out of the trials and tribulations in life. It is offered as a way to lighten life's burdens. Many accept salvation as a luxury or, as described in the audio, a parachute that will improve their flight. Then when life doesn't get better right away or they get mocked for wearing the parachute, they abandon it and end up despising the one who offered it. But the one that is told that salvation is a parachute needed for the jump ahead will hold on to it as a gift.

They will cling on to it awaiting the danger to come, and they will be thankful to the one who offered it to them.

After listening to the audio *Hell's Best Kept Secret,* I realized the method I was using was ineffective in saving the lost. I could totally relate to the parachute story, because that is how I received salvation six to eight times previously. I looked at salvation as a luxury, a way to sin and then get cleansed.

Learning *Hell's Best Kept Secret* has totally changed the way I explain the Gospel to others. If it is your desire to seek and save the lost, then put in the time to learn methods that actually produce results. More importantly, the best way to seek and save the lost is by becoming an example for others to follow. Walk around with an attitude that others will want.

I realize that I can't make someone desire salvation. I can only plant the seeds and water it with the word or through my actions. Remember this, that your life may be the only Bible someone reads or you may be the only Jesus one meets.

Offering Salvation

If I do lead a person into prayer for salvation, I make sure they realize that their job isn't completed. It has just begun. When you accept Christ, you are giving up your life for a life in Christ. "I have been crucified with Christ and I no longer live, but Christ lives in me" (Galatians 2:20). What you have to realize is the Bible has the answers to all of life's problems, but you must read it to find the answers. You can't just hold the Bible in your hand and say, "I'm all good; I have the Bible." You have to read it and let it live through you.

I recommend reading Proverbs first. There are thirty-one chapters, so read one a day. Then after thirty-one days, read them again. Next read the four Gospels: Matthew, Mark, Luke, and John. Those chapters teach you the characteristics of Jesus, the example you want to follow. Then read 1 John. This chapter helps you examine yourself.

This chapter was very important to me. I was saved in August 2007 but was still unsure of my salvation. I began reviewing my life and pondered, *Am I truly saved?* God again answered quickly. He led me to 1 John. It was after reading this chapter that I received reassurance of my salvation.

God is light; in him there is no darkness at all. If we claim to have fellowship with him yet walk in the darkness, we lie and do not live by the truth. But if we walk in the light, as he is in the light, we have fellowship with one another, and the blood of Jesus, his Son purifies us from all sin.

If we claim to be without sin, we deceive ourselves and the truth is not in us. If we confess our sins, he is faithful and just and will forgive us our sins and purify us from all unrighteousness. If we claim we have not sinned, we make him out to be a liar and his word has no place in our lives.
1 John 1:5-10

My dear children, I write this to you so that you will not sin. But if anybody does sin, we have one who speaks to the Father in our defense: Jesus Christ, the Righteous One. He is the atoning sacrifice for our sins, and not only for ours but also for the sins of the whole world.

We know that we have come to know him if we obey his commands. The man who says, "I know him," but does not do what he commands is a liar, and the truth is not in him. But if anyone obeys his word, God's love is truly made complete in him. This is how we know we are in him. Whoever claims to live in him must walk as Jesus did.
1 John 2:1-6

Each time you read the Bible, ask the Holy Spirit to reveal answers to you. Ask the Spirit to show you what you need to know and how you can apply it to your life. Remember knowledge is only as good as the application of what is learned. Since the Bible has all the answers, then make it your life's manual.

Do not leave out the important pieces in your Christian walk. Make sure you allow the Holy Spirit to guide you in your readings. Don't just open the Bible, read a verse, and say job's done. What good is reading the entire Bible if you don't gain any wisdom from it?

Read your Bible then live the Bible. Let the words of the Bible come out of your mouth. Read the Bible and speak of the glory of God. When a problem arises, remember what God says. If you are fearful, say, "For God has not given us a spirit of fear and timidity, but of power, love, and self-discipline" (2 Timothy 1:7 NLT).

When a spirit of lust comes upon you, take every thought captive and say, "That girl is a child of my Almighty Father. I will not dishonor my Father. Holy Spirit, break off any soul ties that may have been created. Forgive me, Lord, for my sins. In Jesus's name, Amen."

Utilize the power of the tongue and speak life, not death.

I Stapled My Thumb

Jesus said, Come follow Me, and I will make you fishers of men.
Mark 1:17

My journey with Christ Jesus continues to be amazing. I relish in His splendor and grace. I am especially fond of how He allows me to understand His Word.

At church, my adorable, adventurous daughter was playing with a staple. Not wanting her to get hurt, I took it from her and put it in my jacket. As I was removing my hand from my pocket, the staple got hold of my thumb. I tried to unhook it with no avail. The more I struggled, the deeper it dug in.

Being a little wimp, I started to cry and laugh at the same time. I was crying because I was in pain. I felt like a fish; the more I struggled the worse off I got. I also started to laugh because it was so foolish. I looked up to my wife with a tear in my eye and said, "Help me!" She came over and freed my thumb. We laughed about it all day. Even as I'm writing this, I'm cracking up.

As a follower in Christ Jesus, I am called to be a fisher of men. Jesus said, "Therefore, go and make disciples of all the nations, baptizing them in the name of the Father and the Son and the Holy Spirit, and teaching them to obey everything I have commanded you. And surely I am with you always, to the very end of the age" (Matthew 28:19-20 NLT).

I've been personally ministering to people and noticed something that relates to the staple story. I've set the bait and have hooked a few people, but they continue to resist the call to follow Jesus. I totally understand; I pushed away God most of my adolescent and early adult life. But as a follower in Christ, I will not give up, because to give up is to allow them to suffer in the eternal Lake of Fire.

I've noticed those who continue to resist Jesus are the same ones that are suffering trial after trial. I'm not saying that following Jesus takes away suffering. What I've learned is that following Jesus lightens the load. The more one struggles with the hook, the worse off they get. Of course, you are to fight on, but why do it alone? Just stop resisting the hook, allow it to take you up on the boat, die to self, and live in Christ (Galatians 2:20).

Our behavior is controlled by two forces: pain and pleasure. We'll do anything to avoid pain and gain pleasure. To die to self and follow Christ means to most pain. They will have to go to church every Sunday instead of watching football, they will have to donate money, they will have to read the Bible, and they will have to follow the Ten Commandments.

Pleasure is to watch the football games all day, chug some beer with the boys, play golf, and just relax. There was definitely a time in my life when I chose football over church, and the times I did go to church, I would check the score on my phone. I once was a holiday Christian (go to church on Christmas, Easter, weddings, christenings).

We must use the two forces of pain and pleasure to our benefit. Instead of looking at following Christ equaling no more fun, look at it this way: to not follow Christ means you have to handle problems alone. To not follow Christ means Christ is not in your marriage. To not follow Christ means your children won't know God. To not follow Christ means you follow Satan. If you follow Satan, you will one day live where Satan lives, the eternal Lake of Fire. In the Lake where "their worm does not die, and the fire is not quenched" (Mark 9:44), "there will be weeping there and gnashing of teeth" (Luke 13:28), "eternal punishment" (Matthew 25:46), "shame and everlasting contempt" (Daniel 12:2), and eternal fire…the blackness of darkness forever" (Jude 1:7, 13 NKJV).

To follow Christ means that your burdens are lightened from you. Jesus said, "Come to me, all of you who are weary and burdened, and I will give you rest. Take my yoke upon you and learn from me, for I am gentle and humble in heart, and you will find rest for your souls. For my yoke is easy and my burden is light" (Matthew 11:28-30).

To follow Christ means He is in your marriage. Christ teaches you how to treat, understand, and more importantly, love your wife. Christ teaches you how to love doing things for her just because He did it for us first.

[Jesus] got up from the meal, took off his outer clothing, and wrapped a towel around his waist. After that, he poured water into

a basin and began to wash his disciples' feet, drying them with a towel that was wrapped around him.
John 13:4-5

When His disciples didn't understand this he explained, "Do you understand what I was doing? You call me 'Teacher' and 'Lord,' and rightly so, for that is what I am. Now that I, your Lord and Teacher, have washed your feet, you also should wash one another's feet. I have set you an example that you should do as I have done for you."
John 13:12-15

To follow Christ means that your children know God. After a ten-mile run, my old knees needed some ice. My two kids came over to me and said, "Daddy, can we pray for your knees?" They prayed and my knees were healed. No ice needed. Glory be to God; my kids know Jesus.

To follow Christ means that you have a relationship with Him and will one day be in heaven. Heaven is described in Revelations:

I saw a new heaven and a new earth, for the first heaven and the first earth had passed away, and there was no longer any sea. I saw the Holy City, the new Jerusalem, coming down out of heaven from God, prepared as a bride beautifully dressed for her husband…He will wipe every tear from their eyes. There will be no more death or mourning or crying or pain, for the old order of things passed away…He who overcomes will inherit all this, and I will be his God and he will be my son."
Revelations 21:1-7

If you're still sitting on the fence, get off and pick a side. Even Jesus said,

I know your deeds, that you are neither cold nor hot. I wish you were either one or the other! So, because you are lukewarm—neither hot nor cold—I am about to spit you out of my mouth... Those whom I love I rebuke and discipline. So be earnest, and repent. Here I am! I stand at the door and knock. If anyone hears my voice and opens the door, I will come in and eat with him, and he with me. To him who overcomes, I will give the right to sit with me on my throne, just as I overcame and sat down with my Father on his throne. He who has an ear, let him hear what the Spirit says to the churches.
Revelations 3:15-22

Praise the Lord for this message and his sense of humor. This story came out of a staple!

To Preach or Not to Preach

In my haste to spread the Gospel (Good News) about Jesus Christ, I've made some errors in my approach to preach. In my eagerness to save the world, I have sometimes failed to read my audience. I quickly learned that not everyone appreciates a preacher. If someone doesn't have a desire to hear the Word, then they will ignore everything you have to say.

Instead of being mad or frustrated, I empathized with them. I understood because I was in their shoes at one point in my life. I pushed away advice from my mom for years. Sometimes when I asked her for advice, I hoped she would just give me advice as a mom, not a woman of God.

My cousin Sam counseled me in my approach to reaching out to others. He told me there is a time to preach and a time to just be a friend. Not everyone wants to hear the Word. Some people just want to unload their burdens.

If you are a friend first, preacher second, you can win more souls for Christ, and that's the goal.

So instead of immediately preaching to my peers, I wait. I ask the Holy Spirit to open a door for me to share my story and then wait.

I've found the easiest way for me to engage someone into listening to my story is telling them I wrote a book. That usually opens a huge door for me to share my story.

Besides sharing your story, the greatest way to share the Gospel is to display Christ in your actions. Walk like Jesus walked. Jesus was a man of love who didn't speak behind peoples' backs. Instead, he uplifted the poor in spirit. Jesus had a servant's heart, as was seen when He washed His disciples' feet. Jesus was a giver, as was displayed when He fed 5,000. Jesus was also a healer that always prayed for the sick. So instead of telling people that you will pray for them later, pray for them right there in their presence so they can feel it.

Dr. Matt was a witness to me. He didn't preach to me. He just showed me how a Christian should act. He uplifted his patients, he taught his patients, and he prayed for his patients. His attitude led me to inquire more about faith. He didn't preach to me; he was just a great role model.

A Silent Father

After graduating high school, I had no idea what I was going to do in life. I just went to community college, mainly to please my parents. I definitely lacked desire and passion toward school, and it was shown in my grades. At one point I had a GPA lower than one. I spent more time playing Dos or Spades (card games) in the cafeteria, or sleeping in the lounge, tired from drinking the night before.

After daydreaming through the first two years of college, I found my calling. I was going to become a millionaire selling long distance. I joined this multi-level marketing company, Excel Telecommunications. I finally found something to be passionate about.

After starting my so-called business, I mustered enough courage to tell my dad that I was going to quit school and focus on my new career. There wasn't anything my dad could say to change my mind. I was going to do this with or without his approval.

Since he realized there was nothing he could say, he told me I had to start making car payments and pay for auto and health insurance. I was now free to make millions.

The millionaire journey wasn't what I expected. I had to get two jobs to pay for my new responsibilities. Freedom, I don't think so! The working part was okay. I enjoyed making money, but all of a sudden, my dad stopped talking to me. He wouldn't even acknowledge me in passing. It was heartbreaking. I guess it was the only way he could express his disappointment.

My Father above uses the same punishment on me when I disobey Him. After sinning, I would always feel a huge separation from Him. My earthly father resumed talking to me once I went back to school. My heavenly Father is the same. He only shows His presence after I repent of my sins and begin obeying His commands.

The Bible says that we are to fear God. I could never understand why I was to be afraid of God. But what I learned is that we shouldn't fear his presence. We should fear his disappearance. Just like a kid lost in a shopping center, the kid fears not having his father's presence.

My earthly father's form of punishment (silence) was the worst kind, and I was fortunate enough to learn from it. I eventually got on track, increasing my GPA to 3.25 plus and graduating from Cal State, San Marcos. Thanks, Dad, for doing what you had to do.

Is God silent in your life? Maybe you knew Him once but got offended by someone at church and bailed. Or you turned from Him so you could enjoy the flashy lights of the world.

If you've been offended, I hope to convey this message: You will be offended. In Luke 17:1 Jesus says, "It is impossible that no offenses should come!" Who more likely to offend you than those that are close to you (church leaders or members, family and friends)? Realize this, that they may be professing their Christianity, but it's their action that is offensive, not the Christ they profess to know.

I pray this, that all those offended will forgive their offenders. You see, when we withhold forgiveness, it is like drinking poison hoping the other person would die.

Remember, forgiveness is not forgetting something happened. Forgiveness is saying, "God, I can't endure this offense. Please take it from me so I can continue to walk in your ways."

If you've turned from Him to go the flashy lights of the world, I want you to consider looking at a lamp or light fixture. Look at how many bugs died once they made it to the light. The things of this world don't satisfy; that's why one continues to seek more: more money, more things, and more relationships. One seeks more because they aren't satisfied. You see, the things of this world just make us thirstier, but the Living Water (Jesus Christ) quenches our thirst.

Enter through the narrow gate. For wide is the gate and broad is the road that leads to destruction, and many enter through it. But small is the gate and narrow the road that leads to life, and only a few find it.
Matthew 7:13-14

Life Is but a Whisper

On January 26, 1986, the space shuttle *Challenger* and seven crew members went up in the sky and exploded a few seconds later. I still remember that day very vividly. We were in our classroom and given the privilege to watch this historic event.

It didn't register right away that all seven astronauts had died. I actually thought B.A. Barraccas from the A-Team would save them from the crash, or Superman would get them out in the nick of time. I imagined them rescued on the ground. How innocent my mind was in the fourth grade.

Three years after the crash a new middle school would be named after the space shuttle. My class would be the first to attend Challenger Middle School.

Within six years of the school's induction, a few people had died from the original class, including one of my best friends, Raymond S. He committed suicide in the tenth grade.

I still remember visiting his body and just waiting for him to jump out and scare me. This was my first experience of death. I left with my friends Archie and Marvin and told them to never make me come to their funeral. I basically told them to not die on me. I couldn't handle another one.

That experience really made me analyze the importance of telling people "I love you" before it's too late. You see, a week prior to Ray's death, I thought about visiting him, but time restraints deterred me. Time prevented me from talking to my dear friend. Maybe he needed to talk and I was supposed to be the one to comfort him.

So if God ever puts a name on your heart, don't hesitate to call and check on them. Buy them a cup of coffee or lunch.

I think this was the point in my life when I started telling my mom and dad I loved them every time I said good-bye, just in case that would be my last chance.

Another guy, John H., was killed while resisting arrest. He was put in a choke hold and died. I remember in sixth grade, on the last day of school, he threw some pastelike material on my arm. He motioned me to rub it off. I did naively, and it grew. He was such a prankster.

The next four that passed away were Ray L., Sherri J., Jennifer B., and Jacob S. By senior year, there was speculation that there was a curse. They called it the Challenger Curse. I had already moved schools by ninth grade, so I didn't really know about the curse until the seventh death. The scary part of the seventh death was that it was almost me.

In June 1993, my cousin Sam and I went over to visit our cousin Mary in San Jose. We drove eight hours in hopes to celebrate the fact that all three of us were graduating high school.

On Saturday evening we were talking in her living room when she excused herself. Minutes turned into hours, and we wondered what happened to her. We went to her room to find out she left to be with her boyfriend, Ron.

Now back to my story. Sam and I were appalled. We traveled eight hours to visit her and she ditched us. She will hate that I am writing this story, but that's what she gets for ditching us.

So Sam, Peter (Mary's brother), and I played cards while contemplating our next move. Peter was too young to go out in the middle of the night, so Sam and I decided to let the cards decide our fate. High card we go home; low card we stick around. It was a high card, so we packed up our bags and headed home.

Sam decided to take the first leg. We talked for a while until I got sleepy. I reminded him to wake me up if he got tired.

So as Sam drove, I was in la la land until I abruptly awoke to a spinning car. Sam had lost control of the car, and we ended up on the other side of the freeway with the tail sticking out into traffic. Relief turned into fear when a semi truck almost collided into us. When Sam saw the truck, he quickly pressed on the gas and avoided the collision.

After the initial shock, we regained our composure and decided to take a break at Casa de Fruita. We figured a nice piece of pie and coffee would set us straight. Pumpkin pie never tasted so good!

After the pie, we continued our journey home. All the way home we talked about life. Our regrets, whom we would have liked to say good-bye to, or dreams of the future. Just six hours of talking about life.

A near-death experience really wakes you up. Tim McGraw said it perfectly in his song "Live Like you Were Dying." I don't recommend trying to die, but one thing you can do is to write out your own eulogy. First write down what you think people would say about you. Imagine your wife, kids, mom, dad, siblings, or friends at the podium speaking about you.

If you are satisfied with what they would say, then good for you. If you can't think beyond a few words, then write about what you would like them to say about you. Then change your life so that it will warrant such praise.

Back to my story. So after hours of talking about life, we arrived at my house. We entered the house, and I immediately hugged my parents and told them I loved them.

My dad approached me and asked if I knew Freddie M. I told him yeah, I went to junior high with him. My dad said, "He died last night in a car accident." I was in total awe. Here I just escaped death only to come home to this story. I later found out about the curse and that he was the seventh.

I always wondered was my life spared from the curse because I moved schools or because Freddie died one hour before my incident. Maybe God wasn't done with me yet. I'm not sure, but I thank God every day that I have the breath of life. If there is anything to be thankful for, choose just the simple things, and life will be just that, simple.

I was Dead on CSI

One of my favorite TV shows was CSI until the show freaked me out. I had borrowed a few seasons from Netflix and would watch it almost daily. During one episode, I paused it to go to the restroom. When I returned from the restroom, I looked at the screen. The scene was a cemetery, and on the tombstone was my name. Now if my name was John or Jack, I wouldn't have blinked an eye, but Orlando isn't a common name. That incident really freaked me out. I stopped watching CSI after that. I wondered if that was a sign. It bothered me for a while. I thought maybe someone was trying to tell me something.

Although scary, sometimes it's important to think about death. How much more would you love your wife if you knew you were going to die tomorrow? Would you really watch that football game instead of playing with your kids? Would you work more or take on a smaller workload? What about salvation? If you were to die tomorrow, would you really turn down Jesus? If not, why wait? Only God knows when our time is up. No person has ever said at their death bed, "I wished I had worked more." So stop putting Jesus on hold. Accept Him, get on the boat, die to self, and live in Christ.

Without love, I am nothing. Jesus's death is the best demonstration of love. He sacrificed His life for us. That's what love is (sacrifice). I've resolved to put aside my desires for my wife's. I'm not saying I give up everything I ever wanted; I just wait until she desires the same thing.

I first present my wishes to God and test it to His word. If it is approved by Him, then I present it to my wife. By respecting my wife's decisions, our love continues to grow. I also have greater joy from receiving my desires, because now it is a gift, a gift from my Father above and my wife.

I was once addicted to football. More like I was addicted to sports gambling. Now that I am delivered from gambling, I don't even bother watching football. Occasionally I watch a few minutes, but the desire is no longer there. Today, my Sundays along with every day belong to the Lord and my wife and kids. Kids grow too fast. I don't want to miss a moment of it. Have you every really looked at your child's face after telling them, "I am busy watching football; I'll play with you later"? It's heartbreaking. So turn off the TV and play with your kids.

Losing my job has to be one of the best things that has happened to me. The event forced Beth and I to really examine our finances and where our money went. After dissecting it, we realized we could survive on less money. Now that we know we can survive on less, I don't need to go out and search for the huge paycheck (another job that would steal time away from the Lord and family). I now can focus on my bookkeeping and speaking business (all businesses that allow me to stay home and watch my kids grow up).

Love, deliverance from strongholds, financial abundance, and salvation are only attainable through Christ. The Bible says, "[Jesus is] the way and the truth and the life. No one comes to the Father except through me" (John 14:6).

Everything comes down to choice. You can choose to say, "That was a great book!" and do nothing, or you can say, "I want what Orlando has!" If you choose the latter of the two, then I applaud your courage, and I offer this prayer for you:

Dear Heavenly Father, thank you for being here in my presence. Please remove the veil of darkness from my eyes and allow the light to come into my life.

[For] God is light; in Him there is no darkness at all. If we claim to have fellowship with him yet walk in the darkness, we lie and do not live by the truth. But if we walk in the light, as He is in the light, we have fellowship with one another, and the blood of Jesus, His Son, purifies us from all sin.
1 John 1:5-7

Again, Lord, I thank you for leading me. I thank you for the strength to accept your calling on my life. In Jesus's majestic, magnificent, glorious name, the name above all names, Amen.

I want to leave you with this last story. Thank you again for reading my book, and I pray that the desire for the Lord is birthed in your heart. I would love to find out what this book did in your life. Please e-mail me at ojavien@gmail.com. Also subscribe to my newsletter, "The Javien Chronicles," so you can receive words of faith, love, and encouragement. You can enter your email address at orlandojavien.com.

An Important Task

Have you ever had something so important to do that you set your alarm on your phone, you put it in your planner, and even wrote it on your hand? It was so important to remember that you even asked a friend to remind you.

Did you forget? Probably not. You didn't give yourself the opportunity to forget.

God has put a task so important on my heart that I did the very thing. On my desk I have it in bold print. I embedded the task on my cell phone screen so as to always remember. It is so important that I'm not giving myself the opportunity to forget.

The task to remember is, "Surrender! Today I die to self and live in Christ."

I must remind myself because I easily forget. It's not the norm. In order for it to be the norm in my life, I must practice; I must make it a habit.

The word *surrender*, or *submit*, has a negative connotation. In wrestling or war, to surrender means to admit defeat. It means to give up control. It is very difficult to give up control since we live in a world that says never surrender. We're supposed to fight, fight, and fight on.

However, by examining the world and all the problems in it (divorce, suicide, murder, alcoholism, and drugs), I've realized that the world doesn't really have anything under control. They actually are controlled by mind-altering devices like TV, the internet, alcohol, and drugs.

So if we were to truly examine what is happening in this world, then trusting or surrendering in Christ is the only way to actually have control. Because when we are alive in Christ, we have the authority of His name to cast out thoughts, urges, and dependencies.

The devil is defeated when you submit to Christ. Submit to the ways of the Lord, and you will be able to experience the joy of the Lord.

We're to submit to the Lord in everything we do (marriage, work, school, and hobbies). God doesn't just want our Sundays; He wants our always.

So throw your hands up in the air and yell out, "I surrender!" Today die to self and live in Christ.

Endnotes

Desire Is Born

1. Jentezen Franklin Ministries Podcast, *Desire* (www.jentezenfranklin.org/podcasts/Desire.mp3) (Accessed September 3, 2008)
2. Jentezen Franklin Ministries Podcast, *Desire* (www.jentezenfranklin.org/podcasts/Desire.mp3) (Accessed September 3, 2008)
3. Rick Warren, *The Purpose Driven Life* (Grand Rapids: Zondervan, 2002), 34.

Bibliography

Arterburn, Stephen, Fred Stoeker, and Mike Yorkey. *Every Man's Battle, Every Man's Guide to Winning the War on Sexual Temptation One at a Time.* Colorado Springs: Water Brook Press, 2000.

Arterburn, Stephen, Fred Stoeker, and Mike Yorkey. *Every Man's Marriage, Every Man's Guide to Winning the Heart of a Woman.* Colorado Springs: Water Brook Press, 2001.

Bevere, John. Enemy Access Denied, Slam the Devil's Door with one Simple Decision. Lake Mary: Charisma House, 1996.

Chapman, Gary. *Five Love Languages, How to Express Heartfelt Commitment to your Mate.* Chicago: Northfield Publishing, 2004.

Comfort, Ray. *The Way of the Master.* Alachua: Bridge Logos, 2006.

Comfort, Ray, and Kirk Cameron. "Hell's Best Kept Secret." http://www.wayofthemaster.com/videolessons.shtml#.

Kendrick, Stephen, and Alex Kendrick. *The Love Dare.* Nashville: B&H Publishing Group, 2008.

Wilson, Eric. *Fireproof, Never Leave your Partner Behind.* Nashville: Thomas Nelson Inc., 2008.

About the Author

Orlando Javien Jr. is a man of many hats. As an entrepreneur, he runs the freelance bookkeeping and tax preparing company, IAMBookkeeper.

By passion he is a middle school religious education teacher, usher and greeter at St. Michael's Church in Poway and a member of the St. Michael's Men's group, Knights of Columbus, Benedictus of San Diego, and Cursillo of San Diego.

Orlando is also an inspirational speaker who loves sharing the lessons he learns from his business life, his faith life and his family life.

As a constant learner of business and entrepreneurship, he shares his knowledge as a networking educator with the global organization BNI (Business Network International).

He has also been blessed to share his faith and life stories to local Rotary and Kiwanis chapters, men's church groups and local high schools.

Orlando is also a YouTube and LinkedIn creator. You can connect with him and view his video content here:

https://www.linkedin.com/in/orlandojavien/

https://www.youtube.com/orlandojavien

If you would like to invite Orlando to speak to your church or business organization, you can contact him at ojavien@gmail.com or his booking agent at https://catholicspeakers.com/profiles/orlando-javien-jr

Orlando's Most Popular Talks Include:

"Do you know Him? How to form an intimate relationship with God."

"God leaves breadcrumbs."

"How to find inner peace in a noisy world"

"How to evangelize with a smile."

"A call to battle: Why men and boys love superheroes."

CPSIA information can be obtained
at www.ICGtesting.com
Printed in the USA
LVHW081124271119
638505LV00003B/479/P